Thanks to: Mike Pink at QPR, Ron Gould for help with photo's and historical research, "Ingham" (not Tony), Simon Skinner, Paul Varcoe, Martin Holland, John Geeves, Geville Waterman and my Dad (without whom I might never have discovered this great club in the first place).

Loftus Road Legends

Volume One

Loftus Road Legends
Volume One

Authors Ron Norris & David Lane

Published by
Woodpecker Multimedia
Suite 6
2 St Johns Road
Hampton Wick
KT1 4AN

Tel (020) 8 255 6560
E-mail woodpeckermultimedia@hotmail.com
Web www.loftusroadlegends.co.uk

ISBN: 0-9543682-1-5

Printed and bound in the United Kingdom

Introduction & Foreword

I am delighted to have been asked to introduce this unique book about Queen's Park Rangers' history - one look at the list of players' names included in the first volume of Loftus Road Legends should be enough to get every Rangers fan excited.

As a player at Loftus Road between 1991 and 1996 I always felt I gave my all, but I certainly wouldn't feel comfortable with the 'legend' tag personally. I appreciate and respect the great heritage of the club I am fortunate enough to manage and along with everyone at Queen's Park Rangers I am working tirelessly towards the day when we can hopefully emulate the successes of the past.

Although this book is predominantly about looking at the achievements and players of yesteryear, I hope you can appreciate that following the club's recent problems I rarely allow anybody to look backwards. One of the fundamental rules that has been established at Loftus Road, from the very top downwards, is to focus on a bright future for our club. We simply can't afford to get stuck in a time warp where we continually look back to the glory days. But in saying that I would hope that the high standards set in the past should be enough to fuel the ambitions of my current squad.

It is very, very important that we can find some new legends for our fans to enjoy and I strongly believe we may already have the makings of one or two here already. In every era we enjoy a new super-hero and I'm determined that my new crop of players will care about the club and will roll their sleeves up for Queen's Park Rangers. The style of leadership I possess is all about banishing greed, complacency and arrogance - replacing them with hard work and humility.

I want to be at Queen's Park Rangers for a long, long time to come and I know one of my first priorities is to get promoted. I firmly believe we have started to put the building blocks in place to achieve that and from there

2002: Queen's Park Rangers Manager Ian Holloway

moving the club that stage further and maybe start challenging for a return to what has become 'The Promised Land'.

To achieve our aims we have to make Rangers a successful business again, hold on to our best players, then, if we do have to sell them for the right price, ensure we have replacements ready to take their place. All the great Rangers teams of the past have been moulded using those principles and that is what I am determined to replicate.

What has helped me in my job is that when we went into administration, we were allowed to keep every key member of the coaching staff in place. In my view that is full credit to David Davies and all those staff who agreed to accept less than the going rate to stay at QPR because they believed in the club. We have all learnt from the mistakes of the past and have come out of administration a stronger club - over our dead bodies will those mistakes be made again.

As a manager all I can ask of the supporters is to stay patient, keep coming along to Loftus Road and to encourage their friends and relatives to join them on match days. There is still some way to go before QPR is fully free of financial restrictions, but with so many other clubs now suffering the same fate, without any shadow of a doubt we have come out of the dark tunnel they are only starting to enter.

I hope you enjoy Loftus Road Legends and the chance to relive the memories of some of the club's finest post-war stars and that you get behind my players as we do all we can to bring the good times back to Loftus Road.

Come on you R's.

Ian Holloway
Queen's Park Rangers Manager

Welcome to the first volume of Loftus Road Legends, a series which will tell Queen's Park Rangers' fascinating history through the eyes of the people who helped make it all happen – the players.

Choosing who to include in Volume One was always going to be a difficult and controversial choice because QPR has a never ending list of names worthy of the "legend" status. So we decided to choose a structured list that not only included as many of the finest players ever to wear our hoops as possible, but equally, players from as many different eras too. Some interviews do overlap, but I'm sure you'll agree that differing views on the same situations make for fascinating reading.

I believe that the players interviewed cover all the key events from Rangers' post-war history. Tony Ingham tells an enthralling tale of football in the fifties, the sixties are well covered by Mark Lazarus and Rodney Marsh, both of whom played key parts in one of Rangers finest moments.

Terry Venables links the sixties to the seventies and from there the baton is taken up by Gerry Francis, Stan Bowles and Phil Parkes. Gary Waddock and Alan McDonald guide us through the eighties, leading neatly into the nineties with Paul Parker and then Les Ferdinand, who discusses those halcyon Premiership years. Ian Gillard completes our twelve players, his story covers a remarkable three decades - having featured for QPR in the sixties, seventies and eighties.

Topics covered include some great chapters in Rangers history; the Cup Finals of 1967, 1982 and 1986, our European campaigns in 1977 and 1985 and of course the fantastic 1975-76 season when QPR came so close to Championship glory. There is so much more but I won't spoil it here, hopefully that's whetted your appetite for what's to follow.

I'm very grateful to all of the players featured for their willingness to talk about their Rangers' memories in such an honest way and I felt that most of them enjoyed reminiscing as much as I was thrilled to meet them.

I hope that fans of all ages will enjoy Loftus Road Legends. Older fans can wallow in a healthy dose of nostalgia and younger fans can learn about QPR's absorbing history straight from the horse's mouths. But whatever your age, I'm sure there will be plenty to appreciate in this book and hopefully plenty that you haven't heard before.

I have to say that this book would have been impossible to complete without the invaluable help of everyone at QPR, especially Mike Pink, whose proactive attitude certainly enhanced Loftus Road Legends.

So, thanks for buying Volume One and I hope you enjoy reading it as much as I enjoyed working on it. If all goes well hopefully there could be a second volume released in 2003.

Come on you R's

Ron Norris

Contents

Ian Gillard gets away from Nottingham Forest's Martin O'Neill

Ian Gillard

**Date: Wednesday 18th September 2002
Venue: The Ely, Blackbush, Surrey
Era: 1968-1982 Appearances: 479 Goals: 11**

Ian Gillard's playing career at the club straddled an amazing three decades, he made his debut in the sixties, was a mainstay at the club through the seventies and still had enough to offer as a player to be able to finish his QPR career in style, at Wembley in 1982. A quite remarkable record.

Ian signed professional forms with the club the season after the League Cup and Second Division double success and made his debut in November 1968. It was the first of well over four hundred appearances for QPR.

Ian enjoyed much success during his time at the club, after taking a few years establishing himself, Gillard went on to become a virtual ever-present for the vast majority of his fourteen years at Loftus Road. He was a key part of the 1975-76 side that came so heart-breakingly close to winning the League Championship and on March 12th 1975, Ian made his full England debut in front of one hundred thousand people at Wembley Stadium. In a match where goals from Colin Bell and Malcolm MacDonald defeated the 1974 World Cup winners West Germany, Gillard did himself proud.

The next season he would be central figure in the UEFA Cup team that famously lost on penalties in the Quarter Finals against AEK Athens in Greece despite winning the home leg 3-0 at Loftus Road.

Just as Gillard's career at QPR was winding down, he enjoyed another exciting and possibly unexpected period of success. Terry Venables had taken over as manager and remarkably Second Division Rangers reached the FA Cup final, pushing Tottenham Hotspur all the way. Defeat in the replay turned out to be his last game for the club, with a young Ian Dawes nipping at his heels, Gillard was granted a free transfer by Venables and moved to Aldershot in the close season. Ian admits he struggled to adapt to football at a lower level, but he helped The Shots to promotion from the basement division prior to the club's financial problems and their ultimate demise.

Ian spent an entire evening talking about his days at Rangers, for which I'm very grateful. He was happy to share his measured, intelligent and honest recollections about his time at the club and it is clear he still cares for Queens Park Rangers deeply.

Ian's loyalty to Rangers is undisputed and his sterling service should never be forgotten by the club's newer supporters or its players - Gillard epitomises an era of loyalty that seems to have vanished from the game.

Gillard is currently kept busy running a successful office cleaning contractors business in Surrey.

Would today's style of football have affected your game if you'd still been playing?

"It definitely would have affected me if I was playing today. I was a full-back and my job was always to defend first, it was as simple as that back then. If you could get forward then it was a bonus but because defenders did just what the word suggests, it meant there were lots of good full-backs around back then because our first priority was simply to defend.

I don't think there are as many good full-backs around these days because they are encouraged to attack so much, they may be quick and athletic but in my opinion they get found out a bit when they're asked to actually defend. I was looking at Ashley Cole during the World Cup, he really is a cracking player, but he's not a good defender. It's not because I'm knocking the lad, he's a very talented player, it's the system he's being asked to fit in to."

As an apprentice at QPR back in the 1960s - how do you feel being a trainee then compares to what the kids do now?

"Judging by what I've seen going around the clubs, and having gone back to QPR, I'd say it's a totally different experience today. We were lucky if we spent one day training a week, the rest was taken up with odd jobs.

We used to spend a lot of our time preparing the pitch, getting it ready for the first team, or cleaning boots and sweeping the terraces. That was a hell of a job, having to sweep up in that old stadium because the terraces were so uneven with big crevices and holes, it was a nightmare job. But now and again, when we were pushing these great big brushes around, we'd find a ten bob note in amongst the rubbish.

So a lot of our time was filled doing heavy work, but it was good in a way because it helped build respect. I don't think today's apprentices have that respect because they have a lot more freedom. I think it made more of a man of you. Being an apprentice was very hard. I remember when we first used to get the chance to train with the first team, we were so excited.

Some people say that we would have been better players if we'd played more football and there maybe some truth in that, but it was Sod's law in a way because that's how the club, and most other football clubs, were run at the time. But in saying that QPR developed a hell of a lot of players from the youth side into the first team, so they must have been getting things right somewhere."

Did you have a lot of interaction with the manager in those early days or were the youth team kept out of the way?

"Oh yeah, Alec Stock was always around, he'd always stop and say hello and I had a lot of respect for the man.

To me he had all the signs of a good manager, because he wasn't just concerned about the first team, he was concerned about the whole club."

What was it like having all those great players around you when you were learning your trade at Rangers?
"Well one particular player helped me a lot, a bloke called Jim Langley. He was in the first team and always had a lot of time for the youngsters.

He played in the same position as me and gave me a lot of advice and encouragement, which meant a lot to me. We used to call him Uncle because he was everyone's friend and was always around to talk to."

After breaking into the first team at QPR you were in and out of the side for two or three seasons. Was that a frustrating time for you as a young professional?
"Yes it was because I kept picking up injuries and wasn't playing particularly well. I got very frustrated with myself.

Gordon Jago turned round as manager one day and said he'd had a couple of offers for me and asked if I'd be prepared to leave. He said the teams were Oxford and Reading and offered me the choice, but then he added, 'or are you prepared to stay at QPR and fight for your place?' I told him I was prepared to stay and fight if he gave me the chance, and in the space of two weeks I was back in the first team.

I told myself that no bastard was going to get back into my position again and I stayed there. After eight or nine games in the first team I was then called up for the England under-23 squad. Something must have sparked me into action and that talk with Jago was the start of it.

But I did go through a long period before that where I was picking up silly, niggling injuries and not performing well. But from that day I don't think I ever looked back and everything seemed to fall in to place.

You need a little bit of luck too, I don't care what anyone says, whether you're the best player in the country or playing Sunday football, you do need luck on your side too."

Do you think the Reading and Oxford moves were bluffs, just a gee up by Jago to see if you were really up for it?
"Possibly, it could have been, but if it was it certainly worked. Jago was another man I respected, he was an honest guy."

Being called up to the England under-23 squad must have felt like a fantastic achievement?
"Yes it did. But the nice thing about it was Gordon Jago came up to me in the players' bar after we'd played Burnley and said 'this has just come

through, you've just been picked for the England under-23 squad'. Which was really nice, I thought it was a lovely touch. The call-up boosted me a hell of a lot."

What did you think Gordon Jago was like as a man?

"I'd say as a man, he wasn't strong enough - but you've got to remember that there were a lot of strong characters at the club at the time. Players like Terry Venables, Alan Harris, Bobby Keetch, Mike Ferguson and Barry Bridges. He couldn't handle that lot.

They were all good players for the club at the time and I think it helped me to be playing with them. But he had the balls to conduct himself in a decent manner even though the late Jim Gregory used to slaughter him. Jago was very polite, a little bit too polite perhaps.

That was the early part of the seventies, but the middle part of the decade was obviously even better for me - after Dave Sexton arrived. He was able to blend the team together and add a few players to the squad."

How did Dave Sexton manage to build that kind of squad with the money that he spent?

"Well it was like pocket money wasn't it? But he blended all the players together and coached us, and without being disrespectful to Liverpool, I think we were the best team in the First Division that season - by far. But if you had a Liverpudlian sitting here right now I'm sure they'd disagree.

I enjoyed that season, not just because of the results, but we played good football and we tried to entertain the crowds too. I think a lot of people respected us for that."

As a young player just breaking into the side could you see the making of the great team QPR were about to become?

"Not at that time, no. When I was just breaking in too many of the team were getting on a bit and nearing the end of their careers - most of the players were only going to be there for a maximum of two years. There was a lot of hassle at the club at the time too.

First of all you had Jim Gregory as Chairman, as you know he would sack managers like nobody's business which creates instability at a club.

So even in the early seventies, when things were going right, the manager only had to make one mistake or say something out of turn and Jim would get rid of him. Certain people tried to get that stability there, Dave Sexton came along and did a wonderful job, but then it's the same old story and he eventually left.

Then we went through another stage of managers coming and going, I think we had four in one season. When Terry Venables arrived stability returned again because Terry knew what 'Slippery Jim' was like. Terry knew what he was doing and he got hold of the club and sorted it out.

Over the years that has been QPR's biggest problem, all that chopping and changing. But to be fair to Jim Gregory he did an awful lot for the club, he made QPR, it's as simple as that.

I used to call him a 'right horrible bastard' to his face and he used to just laugh at me. I had quite a few rucks with him and it wouldn't make a bit of difference. Jim was Jim, but he knew how to run a football club."

I assume you didn't say those things to Jim Gregory the season you broke into the first team?

"[Laughs] No, you're right, it was around 1979 when I was a bit more experienced, when you're younger you have to be a little bit careful what you say. But after a while, when you've got a bit more established and knew how he ticked, then you could let off steam and tell him what you thought. If he kicked me out he kicked me out - it was as simple as that.

But I had time for Gregory, as I said he built QPR, but as a person, man-to-man, he was an absolute arsehole. Sorry about speaking ill of the dead, but he was and he knew what I thought because I could only take so much from him."

How did it feel for players like you, players who obviously worked hard but found it difficult to relate to the Chairman, to hear that Stan Bowles was almost Gregory's best friend and was always being given extra wages and bailed out of different problems by the Chairman? Stan speaks about this in his autobiography, but was it common knowledge with the other players at Rangers at the time?

"Yes it was. It never affected us though. Stan was Stan, we knew he had problems because he was going out with the wrong kind of people, but we accepted it.

I'm not saying it was right that the Chairman was giving him extra money to keep him sweet, but Stan was a loveable guy and everyone got on with him."

So the rest of the first team didn't find it frustrating that they were behaving like model professionals, but someone who wasn't, was being singled out for special treatment from the Chairman?

"Jim liked Stan because he was a real character, he had that little bit of naughtiness about him did Stanley.

Jim liked to be with the players, to be one of the lads, but because he always had more money then us he would always like to come out on top, because he could do.

There was always a lot of banter going on between the players and Jim wanted to be involved with that. If you used to see Gregory in his office he would be sitting there as miserable as anything, but if he was out with the lads he loved it - that was his treat in life.

Jim's release from making money in business was coming to QPR and having fun with the lads, so I can kind of understand why he helped Stan out so much, he liked Stan and wanted Stan to like him.

Jim would see Stan at the ground and say something like, 'how did you get on today Stan, did you win or lose?' Then Stan would feed him a sob story and Jim would sling him some money.

As I say, the players knew it, but it didn't worry us. I felt I was glad not to be in that situation. Dave Sexton knew what was going on too."

The season you made your debut was the season QPR got relegated from the First Division, did the players expect to bounce straight back up to the top flight?

"Yeah, we did. We brought some more players in and we did feel we could return at the first attempt. We knew it was a hard division to get out of though, it always has been and always will be I expect.

I think relegation made more of a man of me though, I grew up very quickly. One minute you're playing against the likes of Jimmy Greaves and George Best, then all of a sudden, they're gone. You're desperate to get a bit more of that action and bounce back as quickly as possible."

In the end it took QPR four seasons, what was the pressure like trying to get back to Division One?

"The pressure was always on the players, but equally the managers and coaches were feeling it too. Jim Gregory obviously wanted to get back as quickly as possible, so the heat was on all the time.

People were getting more and more dejected as time dragged on, but the trouble was we had too many players coming and going I think.

We come back to the same old problem of stability at the club. It wasn't a good time for the players, not at all."

Surely not for you personally though? Didn't Division Two give you the chance to establish yourself in the team and become a far more experienced professional?

"I was fortunate that I was younger and you're right, it did give me the time to get the experience I needed. I seemed to steer clear of injuries then too, which was what I needed.

If I dipped in form, that was down to me, but getting a long injury-free run was essential."

Thankfully we did get promoted back to Division One and we consolidated well for the first two seasons - finishing in mid-table. Then all of a sudden we were title challengers. Did we start the 1975-76 season really expecting to be genuine contenders?

"[Pauses] Yes, we did actually, because the players all had a bet on it. Funny enough it was Stan that started it off and we put a few quid on silly odds of forty or fifty to one.

I think we all had about £10 in each and Stan Bowles took £100 down to the bookies for us.

So we were confident, especially after beating Liverpool 2-0 on the opening day at Loftus Road. Then a couple of weeks later we went up to Derby and won 5-1 without Frank McLintock and David Webb - our two most experienced players.

When you think about that win at the Baseball Ground it was fantastic, we had reserve centre-halves playing against the likes of Roy MacFarland, Colin Todd and Kevin Hector... Derby were a class act and we beat them 5-1. Every time we got the ball forward, we scored.

So we had a good start, then we dipped slightly and went down to about sixth - then of course the long unbeaten run at the end of the season."

Then the heartbreak right at the end?

"Yes... Everyone talks about the Norwich game as the match that blew our chances, but in my eyes it was the re-arranged West Ham game at Upton Park in January [lost 1-0] that did the damage.

We had a couple of injuries and I didn't feel we had to play that game exactly when we did. We did and we lost.

But most people associate our downfall with the Norwich fixture when we went down 3-2.

But you can't knock the run that we had, it was fantastic. Losing once in fifteen games was astounding especially as the majority of those were wins and we were playing against some really great sides."

Where did the belief and confidence come from that year? The previous two seasons we finished thirteenth and fourteenth - those kind of transformations don't seem to happen in the Premiership these days.

"I think it was the way Dave Sexton prepared the team, he was different class as a coach. He instilled belief into us.

Before the season he got us together and said 'right, we're going to do something this season', and we believed it.

I respected the man, as did everyone in the squad. He was a quiet, nice guy - but if you upset him, boy did you know it. You didn't upset Dave, because he knew what he was talking about."

Did Sexton bring any players in that you thought helped transform QPR from a mid-table outfit into Championship contenders?

"We brought in Don Masson and he gave us a good balance in midfield I think. We called Don 'The Fuhrer'.

But the trouble was, with our midfield quartet, we needed four footballs on the pitch. One for Don, one for Gerry [Francis], one for Stan [Bowles] and one for the rest of the team - that was always our joke.

But Don Masson did an excellent job for us and was a good buy, even though he was only ever a short-term signing because of his age. We also had John Hollins and Mick Leach.

Dave Sexton knew how he wanted them to link up with Don Givens and Stan up front with Dave Thomas out wide. I thought the whole team blended in well - not forgetting the best goalkeeper in the country at the time, Phil Parkes."

As a defender it must have been reassuring to have someone like Phil Parkes standing behind you?

"Phil did absolutely magnificently for us. People have tried to knock the team's achievements that season to me in the past, saying things along the lines of 'QPR would have just been a mid-table side without Phil Parkes saving the side'.

But that's a nonsense way of thinking, that's why teams have goalkeepers in the first place - to make saves. I think a great goalkeeper will concede thirty goals less then an average 'keeper over the course of a season.

Phil was obviously a very good goalie and he stopped the ball a lot better than most - every great team needs a good 'keeper."

There were certainly a lot of characters in Sexton's runners-up team.

"You're right there were so many big personalities in the team. There was a lot of piss-taking that used to go on, but nobody took offence because everyone had strong characters - there was a lot of togetherness."

It must be difficult because there's a lot to choose from, but can you pick a favourite game from that season?

"I think the best game we played that season was away at Newcastle near the end of the season. There were about 45,000 Geordies there that night and about 200 QPR fans. I remember they had us on the rack for about half an hour and Newcastle went one-nil up. Then we got out for the second half and we absolutely slaughtered them.

I know Stan had a bet with Newcastle's Malcolm Macdonald about who would win the match - in fact it was Macdonald who had scored the opener. But we pulled the game back to one-all, then right near the end Stan scored the winner. There was a photo hanging up at Loftus Road somewhere showing Stan gesticulating to Macdonald after that goal.

There were so many great games that season, but that one still stands out to me because the Newcastle fans were absolutely dying for us to lose and when Stan stuck the ball in the net for the winner the place went silent. Our performance in the second half was absolutely superb, we stunned the Geordies."

For some reason Liverpool were allowed to complete their last fixture a week later and QPR had to wait to find out if they were League Champions or not. How did it feel waiting for that result?

"Well, the first team all went to Israel for a five day break before coming back to play Mick Channon's testimonial match. But the waiting around was soul destroying.

The players were all invited in to the TV studios to watch the Liverpool game live, a few went along, but most couldn't face it to be honest. I went out of the house and tried to go missing while the game was on. I didn't want to know the score so I went down the pub. I was only in there about fifteen minutes when this guy came over and told me the score.

I couldn't believe it, that was the real low of my career. People talk about the feeling of getting into the Cup Final, but in the League, to get that close to winning, you've got to be consistent for nine months, week in week out.

If you get beaten once, you've got to bounce straight back, like Liverpool did year after year after year. We had one season and missed out which I feel completely destroyed us.

It hit us bad and we couldn't handle it, which became clear at the start of the next season."

Two years after that QPR got relegated again, was that solely because of the club's Championship hangover?

"Well we had a decent run in the UEFA Cup the season after missing out and we played well in a lot of the European matches, but our League form really dipped.

Dave Sexton was frustrated which led to a lot of barnies between him and Gregory I think - then Sexton left and we became unstable again. I felt the club was in turmoil, I just didn't know what was happening."

The run in Europe must have helped you develop even more as a player though?

"It did, yes. But as I said, it was frustrating too as we were scoring lots of goals in Europe without achieving any consistency in our League form.

Maybe we were concentrating more on Europe than we should have been? One season you're right up there with the best in the land, then the next you're losing a lot and just floating around.

I think the final straw was when we played AEK Athens, we beat them at home 3-0 and thought we'd finished the tie off already.

Then we went over there and they gave us the biggest pounding you could ever imagine - they pulled it back to 3-3, took the tie to extra time, then did us on penalties."

Everybody tries to compare Bowles and Marsh, having played with both while you were at the club, how do you compare the two?

"To me there is no comparison. They both possessed an awful lot of skill, but the difference was that Stan was a team player and Marshy was for Marshy.

Obviously Stan did his own individual thing on the pitch, but he worked hard for the team too.

I always found Marsh a little reluctant to help the younger players too, Stan was the complete opposite in that respect."

Did you read both of their autobiographies?

"No. I read Stan's but not Rodney's."

You won three full international caps for England while you were at QPR, do you think you deserved more?

"I was very fortunate in some respects, but I also achieved a lot of bad publicity about my call-up for England. I remember a journalist wrote in one of the national 'papers about five years ago that he thought I was the worst England left-back ever.

Everyone has got their own opinions, but there'd be something wrong with me if I told you I wasn't hurt by that. Okay, I was fortunate that two very good players got injured, Alan Kennedy and Kevin Beattie, but I was over the moon to be called into the squad but I didn't think I'd play.

But Don Revie picked me and I started against the World Champions Germany, we beat them 2-0 in front of 100,000 people at Wembley. I thought I'd performed well on the night, I certainly didn't disgrace myself.

In the second game, against Wales, I don't think I played particularly well, but I took a lot of flak for the game that we lost 2-1 in Czechoslovakia. The Czech winger Marian Masny was very tricky, I could have played better, but again, I don't think I let anyone down.

But to answer the question, I couldn't really say that I justified any more caps and I was fortunate that other players were injured allowing me to be called up. That's all I can honestly say about the situation, I'm very,

very proud to have represented my country and nobody can take that away from me."

What did you feel your relationship was like with the fans while you were at Rangers?
"I think I've always got on well with the supporters. Obviously there were one or two comments shouted at me from the terraces now and again, but football wouldn't be football without those."

You said that you played under something like sixteen different managers while you were at QPR, who was your personal favourite?
"Dave Sexton stands out I think. I was lucky to play for some real characters though, my first manager was Alec Stock who was an Alex Ferguson-like man who did a lot for me as a youngster. But Dave Sexton was the main man. Obviously I thought a lot about Terry Venables too, he was a nice bloke, he was easy to talk, I have a lot of respect for Terry."

Are there any who you didn't get on quite so well with?
"Tommy Docherty I suppose, the second time he was at the club. I was just a kid in his first stint at QPR and he gave me my League debut so I thought he was fantastic, but he was a nightmare when he came back.

On the one hand he was a bundle of fun, but he couldn't handle senior pros. When you're that little bit older and that little bit more experienced you see things very differently.

Docherty once dropped our goalie because he found out he had a better Jaguar than his own."

But were you looking forward to seeing him come back when you first heard the news and after what you remembered about him as a youngster?
"Not really, no. I'd matured and wised up by that stage. As I say, he was a superb entertainer, but for Queen's Park Rangers he was a complete nightmare to be honest.

He nearly ruined a few players actually. He brought a lot of young players into the club, paid them double what the senior professionals were on and made us train on our own for absolutely no reason. There was a lot of unrest and upheaval."

So you were happy to see Docherty given the boot at the end of the 1979-80 season?
"Well there were a lot of players that liked Docherty and when they heard that Gregory had sacked him they called a meeting to try and get him

reinstated. I told them that I didn't want to get involved, but in the end I went along. I remember calling Gregory up on behalf of the senior players as they could only get through to Jim's secretary, but I was getting fed up because I didn't want to spend my time trying to reinstate the man.

Anyway, I rang Gregory up and said to his secretary, 'put the old man on, tell him who it is', and he spoke to me. I told him what the situation was from the senior pros' point of view and he told us he wanted us to come in and see him. In the end Docherty was reinstated, but after about three months, was sacked again. So it achieved absolutely nothing!"

Your last games for QPR were the FA Cup Final and Replay against Tottenham, it must have been good to bow out in style. What do you remember of the cup run 1982?

"We had a certain amount of luck I think. We struggled to get a draw against Middlesbrough at home, then went up there, battled away and won. We went to Blackpool in the next round, struggled again, got a draw, then murdered them in the replay.

Then we got a bit of extra belief and confidence from being in a run - but you can't get to the Cup Final without luck.

It was the same against West Brom in the Semi-Final, we were just hanging on at one stage. Clive Allen had done nothing all match, then all of a sudden, in the 80th minute he pops one in and Rangers are at Wembley.

In the first game against Spurs I thought they deserved to win, but our 'keeper Peter Hucker was outstanding - he kept us in it and we got a second bite at the cherry.

In the second game I thought we did pretty well even though we didn't really look like scoring. One or two half chances, but it was our play in the final third of the field that let us down. But when you're in a Cup Final you hope and pray that you get the chance that goes in.

I think we took a lot of credit out of those two matches because we contained Spurs well for a Second Division outfit.

But it all goes so quickly, you try and take it all in, absorb all the sights and sounds, but you're in and out almost as quickly as you can say 'Jack Daniel's'. Getting to the Cup Final wasn't the same feeling as in 1975-76, not the same feeling at all. Missing out on the League Championship was far more disappointing."

On Cup Final day does your mind wander back to 1982?

"Yes, always. Sometimes my missus says 'get your video out and watch the QPR Final', but I just can't watch it.

I have certain flash-backs from time to time when I'm watching a game on TV, nutmegging Paddy Roche in goal for Manchester United at Loftus

Road pops up a lot. But if I'm watching football with my son, memories flood back all the time when I look at the grounds on the telly."

What made you stay at QPR for virtually your whole career? I assume you must have had opportunities to move on.

"I was always happy at QPR really, I liked the club and I liked the people there. I think things were different back then, if you were happy with what you were doing, you stayed.

Since I've been out of the game, though, I've met managers who've told me that they tried to buy me at certain points and you think, 'oh yeah, why didn't you say something to me at the time!' But there were no agents and there was no tapping up back then.

I found out that Millwall were interested and approached Terry Venables when he was manager. There was supposed to have been a chance to have gone and played for Vancouver Whitecaps, but most of it was hearsay.

At the end of the day I was happy at the club and I enjoyed it, so there was no reason to go."

So what happened at the end?

"Just before the Cup Final Terry Venables called me into his office and told me that he was dropping me for the away game at Luton that night. He said he wanted to give someone else a go and that he was going to give me a free transfer at the end of the season. I said 'okay fine, if that's what you want to do'.

It hurt me quite a bit because I wanted to stay there, perhaps not as a player, but QPR was in my blood. I'd spent a hell of a lot of time there, 1966 to 1982, my whole adult life.

Even if I go and watch QPR now I still feel that I am part of the club, it may be a silly thing to feel, but after sixteen years you can't help feeling you've got that connection."

1967: Rodney heads towards goal watched by Mike Keen

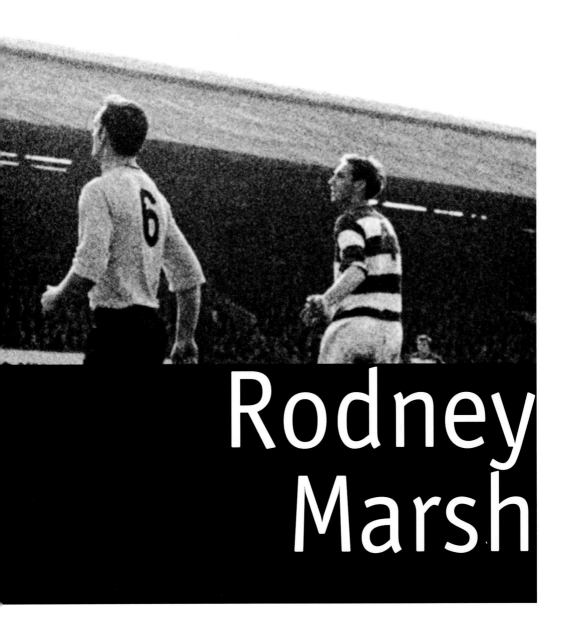

Rodney Marsh

**Date: Monday 19th August, 2002
Venue: BSkyB Studios, Isleworth
Era: 1966-1972 Appearances: 242 Goals: 134**

Rodney Marsh is an enigma, a man whose reputation precedes him. The fact that he is one of the greatest footballers this country has ever produced is something that has almost been forgotten. Now he is Rodney Marsh, controversial TV pundit and fan of his own opinion, but for many QPR fans he is arguably the greatest Rangers legend of them all.

Forty-four goals in one season, scorer of the finest goal ever seen at Wembley and part of the only QPR side to win anything. Ask any R's fan who was watching in the late sixties and early seventies and they will go misty eyed at the thought of our 'first great number 10'.

Rodney arrived for £15,000 from Fulham on the transfer deadline day in March 1966 and considering that he was The Cottager's top scorer the season before with 18 goals, the deal emerged as one of the biggest bargains in Rangers' history. Marsh would go on to enjoy six glorious seasons at Loftus Road and make his name in the game.

It's sometimes difficult talking to ex-players who've been 'asked it all before', but this interview turned out to be anything but regurgitated reminiscing - although it was approached with caution. For some reason I got the impression that Rodney's TV persona was not so much a well crafted public image, more Rodney just being himself. I think I was right.

Rodney just "tells the truth" and as he says this can upset people - so for the first few minutes I thought it was going to be a disaster. But then something clicked and he started to warm, suddenly the answers were flowing, his opinions forthcoming and there was a passion in his voice.

As it transpired he was an absolute pleasure to speak with and it became obvious that Marsh has a great and genuine fondness for Queen's Park Rangers - more so than I ever expected in all honesty.

From humble beginnings in London's East End, Rodney has built a life outside football more successful than perhaps even he could have dreamed of and good luck to him.

But for QPR fans it's the years he graced the pitch at Loftus Road with such style and panache that will live long in their memories. Rodney's status as a definitive Rangers icon is unquestionable and assured for a very long time to come.

As you'll will no doubt discover, virtually everybody featured in this book has an opinion on Rodney Marsh, but whatever his peers thought of him as a person, not one doubted his ability on the football pitch.

When you arrived at QPR in 1966 did it feel like you were joining a club on the up?

"Very much so, and that was down to the chairman at the time Jim Gregory. He had great vision about the future of QPR, he was such a passionate man and he was one of those people who put his money where his mouth was. He had the vision to take the club forward. Not dissimilar to what Al-Fayed has done with Fulham really."

We won the league that year by twelve points when there were only two points for a win, scoring over 100 league goals in the process. Just how good a side did we have?

"It's hard to make modern day comparison and analogies but I would say that it was one of the most exciting teams I have ever seen, ever, and I've watched football for a long, long time.

We played the old WM formation, so we had goalscoring wingers in Morgan and Lazarus, two goalscoring strikers in myself and Les Allen, complemented by two midfield workhorses in Mike Keen and Keith Sanderson. It was a fantastic side."

I read that you rated Les Allen as the best strike partner you ever had, why was that?

"People never really give enough credit to Les Allen. He was an outstanding footballer, with a great football brain. He could score goals, make goals, he had great vision and never ever got the credit he deserved. He was absolutely top drawer."

Do you think you took the limelight away from Les?

"In some ways I suppose I did, maybe he got the hump about that, I don't know."

We really trounced some teams during 1966-67, seven-one at Mansfield, six-nil against Doncaster. Do you have a personal favourite league game from that season?

"My favourite game was actually from the year before, when we played Millwall and beat them 6-1 - I scored two and made three. I always remember that game as being absolutely incredible, it was just wave after wave after wave of attack. We scored six but it could easily have been sixteen."

From your point of view was the match against Millwall a perfect personal performance?

"No actually, that came in a game just after we won the League Cup. We played Bournemouth at Loftus Road, that for me stands out as the most

The young Rodney Marsh became Rangers' first great number ten

perfect game I ever played. I think I only scored two or three but it was one of those games where they couldn't get the ball off me. You have those from time to time and I played the perfect football match."

Talking of the League Cup Final, I think people might be a little blasé about it now as the competition has been so devalued. For the benefit of younger readers can you tell us just how much of an achievement it was for Rangers to win the League Cup that season?

"Well at the time it was staggering because people thought of it as being a big competition. We beat West Brom, who in those days were a top First Division team. To put it in today's terms you could compare them with Newcastle or Leeds, plus we were two-nil down at half time of course!

So for a Third Division team to come back and win three-two against a team like that, in front of one hundred thousand people, in the first Wembley Final was an incredible achievement. Absolutely incredible."

Did we always believe we could win at Wembley?

"Well in those days we had a manager called Alec Stock and he only knew one way to play which was all out attack. We didn't change our system home or away. It helped that we had players at the back like Frank Sibley, who was a tremendous defender, so not only could we go forward but when we were under the cosh we could defend well too."

Should your overhead kick in the Final have been allowed?

"No, it was offside! I didn't realise it at the time, in the heat of the game you just put it in the net and ask questions afterwards, but I was about three yards offside."

Your equaliser has been described as one of the greatest goals scored at Wembley, what can you remember about it?

"It was one of those 'no-brainers' really, I picked the ball up about forty-five yards out and I just wandered around with the ball until I saw a gap. I hit it into the space and it cannoned off the inside of the post and smashed into the net. I don't actually remember too much about it, it was one of those instinctive goals you score from time to time."

What are your thoughts on Stan Bowles, can you compare yourselves as players?

"I think it's very difficult to compare players from different generations, but I will say that Stan Bowles was one of the most talented footballers that I ever saw. He was a fantastic player with incredible skill. The only reason I think the team that played before Stan gets so much recognition

1968: Marsh against Huddersfield at Loftus Road in a 3-0 win

is because we won things and achieved so much. We won the Third Division Championship, the League Cup and of course we got promoted to the First Division the year after that.

All those things came in only a couple of years, we were winning things and scoring millions of goals and QPR haven't won much since.

When you look at the team I played in we scored over a hundred goals and our main forward player, me, scored forty-four in one season. That makes it much more difficult for the teams that follow to come up to that standard. So when you are comparing players and teams from different times it's very difficult."

Why didn't you get into English football management?

"I never really fancied it, I've never really wanted to manage or coach in this country. I did in America for ten years with the Tampa Bay Rowdies. I played there, coached, then managed before finally becoming their Chief Executive. But I never wanted to manage in England because of the way they are treated in this country by the tabloid press and by the fans. I wouldn't want the aggravation that goes along with the job."

When you were in discussion for the Chief Executive's position at QPR in the early nineties could you already see the problems at Rangers which would ultimately lead to our collapse?

"No is the short answer! A lot of people were anti Richard Thompson at the time but I always found him to be an extremely astute businessman and a very clever man too. I certainly didn't see the demise of QPR, all I saw was potential success.

QPR's collapse coincided with Richard Thompson leaving the club and Chris Wright taking over. You couldn't predict it at that time and I don't think you can blame Richard Thompson for what happened after he left."

After the job offer was withdrawn your reputation took a bit of a battering amongst Rangers fans - was that unfair on you?

"I did take a battering yes. The problem is people are offended by the truth sometimes. I told the absolute truth about the situation at the time and when I'm asked now I tell the absolute truth. I don't bullshit and if people don't like the truth then fuck them."

I think at the time people thought you were trying to muscle in on Gerry Francis, but after reading your autobiography that doesn't seem to be the case.

"Well I told the truth at the time, I told it in the book and I'll tell it to you again now. The first thing I said to Richard Thompson was before we do anything I want to meet with Gerry Francis. That was the first thing I said, so how in the world that ever got misinterpreted I don't know."

You stated a couple of seasons ago that Rangers were heading for the Conference if they didn't sort themselves out.
"Yes, I was right as well!"

Do you feel the club has turned the corner now?
"Well twelve months ago it was desperate times, the club almost went out of existence let alone the Conference. I think I was right when I said that, but a lot of people at the time were offended by my comments.

QPR supporters wrote to me saying how disloyal I was for saying that. I think I was spot on, but people got offended by the truth then as well.

My understanding is there still isn't an awful lot of money within the football club. Once you start losing players because of financial reasons then who's going to come and play for you when the players you have aren't good enough to go somewhere else.

I think QPR have turned the corner in terms of steadying the ship - it's stopped sinking but it's still treading water."

Does it hurt you to see Rangers back in the position they were when you joined them?
"That's my most asked question and I give the same answer every time. People are always willing to have a chip at me when I say something negative but never compliment me when I say something positive, so I'll say it again now. 'I love QPR'.

When I arrived they were a Third Division team drawing about four thousand people, when I left they were at the top of the tree, getting about twenty thousand people and playing great football. I always look at QPR as being my club, if people ask me 'who's your favourite club?', I say QPR."

Were you asked to become involved with any take-over bids prior to Queen's Park Rangers' administration?
"I chatted with a couple of guys about it, they came down to see me at a club I go to in London. I spoke to them for about an hour and they were asking my opinion on what I thought.

The thing that hit me was it really wasn't organised properly. They didn't show me a three-year or five-year plan, they just wanted my help to get some money.

That bothered me a bit, when I was with the Rowdies we had short term and long term goals - clear thinking about what we were trying to achieve. I don't think they had that.

They were very passionate, but usually if you meet with someone you say 'this is what we are trying to do' and 'this is what we want to achieve'. When you are doing that sort of thing you really need a plan.

I was approached by the Fulham 2000 fund a couple of years ago and they were similar - passionate people who care and want to help - but didn't have a plan as to what they were doing."

How do you feel Ian Holloway is performing as manager?

"I think he is doing very, very well with extremely limited resources. He's the sort of person that will dig his heels in and he will graft. I think he's doing well with what he has got but it would be a difficult job for anybody. I'm not one of these people that criticise him, I don't agree with the people that do that. I've read some articles in the 'papers where people were having a bit of a chip at him, but I don't agree with that."

Do you feel today's QPR can emulate the QPR of 35 years ago?

"That's a bit of a stretch! I personally think that the QPR team I played for was the best QPR team of all time. I know that the seventies team with Gerry Francis, Stan Bowles and Frank McLintock were good as well and almost won the First Division but I always look at the team I played in as a magnificent football team.

We had so much quality throughout the side in all positions, we won so much and we won with flair.

They were great days for me. I moved on to Manchester City who were one of the biggest teams in Europe at the time, but I always look at that team as being special - very special. So today's team would have to do a lot to emulate my team!"

Paul Parker

Date: Thursday 10th October, 2002
Venue: Writtle Sports Ground, Chelmsford
Era: 1987-1991 Appearances: 156 Goals: 1

Paul Parker was only at QPR for a relatively short period of time, so it is testament to the man that he cemented his place in Rangers folklore inside just four years.

Paul joined Queen's Park Rangers from neighbours and local rivals Fulham after the collapse of the proposed merger between the two clubs in 1987. He proved a fantastic signing for the club and Jim Smith and Peter Shreeves helped transform a promising young pretender into arguably one of the best defenders to ever pull on a QPR shirt.

Parker was virtually an ever present in his first three seasons at Rangers and helped QPR finish in fifth place, as top London club, in his debut year. In the 1989-90 season he would also be a part of the Rangers side that, despite having to endure countless replays, earned a place in the FA Cup Quarter-Final where they were narrowly beaten by Liverpool in yet another replay.

By this stage Paul had already made his full England debut and that summer would prove to be perhaps the highlight of his career. He was a regular in the England side that famously reached the World Cup Semi-Final in Italia '90 and came so close to getting even further.

Everyone remembers Paul's involvement in 'that' deflected goal, something he still gets stick about, but nether the less, it was a very proud achievement for both Paul and for Queen's Park Rangers - not to mention England as a nation.

In the summer of 1991 Paul was sold to Manchester United for a (then) record fee of two million pounds. At Old Trafford Parker went on to win two Premier League Championships and an FA Cup winners' medal - so you may find it a little surprising that such a decorated footballer should be found on a cold, muddy field in a tiny little village called Writtle on the outskirts of Chelmsford in Essex.

Paul is now trying to forge a new career for himself in the game and is the manager of Dr. Marten's Premier League outfit, Chelmsford City. Parker is using his contacts within football to build an impressive young side, but only time will tell whether his fledgling managerial career can emulate what he achieved on the football pitch as a player.

I found Paul to be an instantly likable person and whilst his time at the club was not covered in the medals and honours he would enjoy later, it was evident that Rangers is still very close to his heart.

You joined Rangers in 1987, that was the start of an amazing period in your career wasn't it?

"Coming to Rangers changed my life really, the best thing I could have done was to move from Fulham to QPR. At the time Fulham was a small time operation and when I arrived at Loftus Road I realised I'd joined a big club.

I really thought I'd made it, no disrespect to Fulham, but I couldn't believe the difference. Fulham is totally different now though, it's just a rich man's club, I don't look at Fulham with any warmth now or feel it's the club where I grew up at any more."

You'd been highly rated for quite a while before leaving Craven Cottage, you maybe stayed there longer than some people thought you should have?

"That was down to naivety more than anything else. I'd grown up with a lot of the people at the club and they were my friends, people like Dean Coney. I'd been playing with him from the age of ten. At the time I didn't really have the vision to move on or try myself at a higher level. Fulham upped my money whenever they needed to and I was happy to stay I guess. When I got a bit older and started to pay more attention to what was written in the 'papers, I started to realise there was more to life than Fulham.

What capped it for me was when Ernie Clay [ex-Fulham Chairman] turned down £200,000 from Liverpool for me just after we'd taken them to three matches in the Milk Cup, I then realised that I wanted to move on. Obviously my move to Rangers came about under the cloud of merger between Fulham and QPR and about £350,000 was paid for both Dean Coney and myself.

I've got Jim Smith to thank for the move. I look upon Jim Smith and Alex Ferguson as the two major people in my career for what they did for me. One got me into the top league in the country and the other took me to the biggest club in England.

It was good to be able to move with Dean Coney as we'd been together for so long, but I knew a few of the other lads from playing in West London. I'd played against Alan McDonald, Wayne Feraday, Warren Neill and Gary Waddock when they were in the youth team. But by the time I arrived they'd been playing in the top flight for a few years and had a big head start on me."

Did it boost your confidence to arrive at Loftus Road?

"I can remember Peter Shreeves telling me when I first arrived: 'we've signed you because you're quick and you can defend. You can't pass the ball though, so when you get it, give the ball to Kevin Brock because he can'. At the time it hurt, but I laugh about it now and it's something I tell my players about now that I'm managing Chelmsford City. Ultimately taking Shreeves' advice on board is what made me really, I was a man-marker and I made my name at QPR. Playing alongside Alan McDonald and Terry Fenwick was great for me too.

Fenwick was a good leader and Macca was a good person to have around because he was so honest - his fitness wasn't the greatest but if you needed someone to 'do or die' there was nobody better. I knew when I was playing centre-half with Macca that anything played up the side, I did the chasing, I did all the running for him. In return, anything in the air or when someone needed to stick their head in where it hurt, I could always count on Macca. [Laughs] At the end of the day he couldn't make his face worse than it was anyway."

You seemed to adapt to the higher level very quickly?
"It was all down to Jim Smith and Peter Shreeves, as I said, their advice made me keep things simple and it proved to be effective. I was marking the likes of John Fashanu, Tony Cottee and Graham Sharp every week and because all that was expected of me was to stop them getting past me, win the ball, then lay it off to someone else, it took a lot of pressure off me.

I think the plastic pitch helped me a lot too. I was reasonably quick and I knew not many people could beat me, but with the pitch there was a good chance the ball would run on further and my pace would help me even more than on grass. The pitch didn't help my body though, Christ, did you get some scars! I've still got burn marks on my elbows, knees and on the sides of my hips."

Do you remember much from your debut?
"It was against West Ham United and I was marking Tony Cottee. I was delighted, they ended up taking him off and we won 3-0 at Upton Park. That suited me down to the ground because I was born near West Ham and absolutely hated them as a club because of the racist elements at the time. In fact I never lost at West Ham as a player."

In your four seasons at Rangers you played under three different managers. Was there too much chopping and changing going on at the club?
"I was gutted when Jim Smith went, the same with Peter Shreeves - he was one of the best coaches I've ever played for. His manner made you want to do well for him, he would ask you to do things and if you didn't do what he wanted he would make you feel disappointed that you'd let him down. People say that everywhere he's been.

I got on well with Trevor Francis too, but where it went wrong with Trevor was a lot of players thought they were still friends with him when he took over as manager - they didn't adapt to him becoming their boss. When that happens, as a player, you must accept that relationships change.

The Martin Allen incident didn't help Trevor either - even though I thought Francis was right. Regardless of the situation I think Martin left the rest of the team in the lurch with what he did, okay his wife was pregnant but she was in good hands, it was nothing serious and there was a game on. Martin Allen should have talked to Trevor before just vanishing and I'm sure he would have been allowed to return home with the manager's blessing. Instead he just left a message with another player, checked out of the hotel at 6am and let his team down. All the women's magazines getting involved didn't help Trevor's position either and I think that problem still haunts him today.

After Trevor came Don Howe, which was good for me personally - Don got me to the World Cup in 1990. Considering I was at 'unfashionable Queen's Park Rangers' and was having to have cortisone pain-killing injections in each thigh before I played, the important thing was that I had been introduced to the England set-up because of Don.

But for some reason Don's attitude to me changed after the World Cup, that gutted me. When I got back from Italia '90 Don started calling me a 'Big Time Charlie', I don't think I deserved that, I thought he was making me out as something I wasn't.

I've never forgotten where I've come from and I lost it a bit after that."

It was about that time that you badly injured your knee?
"Yeah, in the stupid Zenith Data Cup at Southampton in front of about 5,000 people. I didn't want to play in that game really, but Don made me.

Rangers' Physio, Mike Varney, did a great job on me though, he was different class. I was having to drive in every day for treatment from Billericay to the training ground at Hanger Lane, I was stuck in traffic all the way in and all the way back driving with a bad knee and it was doing me in.

Mike then suggested I started going to his clinic in Enfield instead as he had all the right equipment there and I did all my fitness training with his son, who was a deep sea diver. When I came back I thought I was as fit as I'd ever been.

I remember playing at Old Trafford with skin diver's shorts under my kit and Mark Robins turned me and struck this unbelievable shot. I knew that if Robins could beat me for pace then I couldn't have been as fit as I thought, but I carried on and got my match fitness back. That was my last season at Rangers."

Which manager do you think you played your best football for while you were at Rangers?

"I'd say Jim Smith because I had the passion and desire to go out and prove something. I wanted to play in the First Division and I had the right appetite for it. That was a good time to be playing for QPR, alongside people like Mark Dennis and Gary Bannister - he was the most under-rated centre-forward I ever played with.

I've still got a lot of good friends from my time at Rangers too, Peter Reid, Nigel Spackman, Colin Clarke, Ossie Ardiles and Ray Wilkins. Just think about it now, quality like that on the same pitch. Today, a lot of people would think it wasn't possible for all those players to have turned out for Queen's Park Rangers. It was incredible, between 1988 and 1989 Rangers had some fantastic talent at the club."

Do you remember your goal?

"[Laughs] What my only ever goal for QPR, against Luton Town? I think you'll find that was one of the greatest goals that Loftus Road has ever witnessed. Yeah, I remember it, I played a one-two with Andy Sinton in a 6-1 win and shot it across the 'keeper - no great pace but a bit of a Jimmy Greaves finish even if I do say so myself.

The funny thing about it was Luton's manager at the time, Jim Ryan, became the reserve team manager when I was at Manchester United and we got talking about that match after he arrived. He said the worst thing about losing 6-1 that night was the fact that I scored a goal because in his team talk before the game he'd told the Luton players not to worry about me coming forward. But we must have been pretty comfortable in the match for me to venture the other side of the half-way line."

We got to the Quarter Finals of the FA Cup in 1989-90, but to get to that stage we had to play Cardiff twice, Arsenal twice, Blackpool three times and eventually went out to Liverpool after another replay. How did those extra ten games in just six weeks affect the players?

"I would say that all the talk today is about squad rotations and players needing rests, but as far as I was concerned if I had a midweek game that was absolutely perfect.

I knew that if we were playing on Tuesday night after a game the previous Saturday, we'd only have a stroll in training on Monday, then we had the game on Tuesday. We would get a day off on Wednesday, not have to work that hard in training on the Thursday because of the game the following Saturday, we'd have to come in on Friday but only for a five-a-side or a few sprints - then we'd play on Saturday. Basically, I didn't want to train, I just wanted to play.

Speaking with an English player's mentality, if you play forty-two games per season then squeeze in another ten to fifteen cup matches on top of those, then you'd want to play in them and not be rested. Most players I know want to be in the team at all times and don't like being rotated. They want to be involved in the side every match day, they want to be in the players' bar after the game with the rest of the first team.

There was nothing worse during my last year at Manchester United [1996-97] when I lost my place after having an ankle operation and they were winning games week in week out. You'd go in the players' lounge at Old Trafford after the game and because you hadn't played you couldn't get involved in all the chat. None of your friends wanted to come up to the games because you weren't playing, it's the worst feeling in the world when you're not involved. To be left on the outside looking in isn't good at all, so you want to play in as many games as you possibly can."

When you first got selected for the England squad at QPR, how did you hear about it?

"I remember being told by the manager the morning the squad had been named and a letter arrived the next day confirming it. From that day on, whenever the squad was announced, I would rush out of training and get back to the car to get the radio on and see if my name was in it. After having a shower you'd be trying to get dressed before you were dry.

I think the England squad almost picks itself these days because of the amount of foreign players in the game, but back then there was always a bit of uncertainty and you would be itching to find out, it was exciting but worrying at the same time."

How did you find the step up to International football?

"It's so different to league football, it really is. I remember my first start was against Denmark over in Copenhagen, I got the ball at right back and thought 'this is easy'. I grew in confidence, but then made the fatal mistake of overlapping with Chris Waddle in midfield and found myself in the final third of the pitch. All of a sudden I thought a forest had gone up before me and I panicked. I couldn't comprehend all those defenders in front of me. In that split second I learnt an awful lot about International football, unless you are good enough you don't want to be playing any more than three touches on the ball.

When I was at Manchester United people always said to me 'Paul, you never do anything, you just get the ball and pass it... you don't do any-thing'. I used to tell them that I couldn't do any more than that!

I was just a small cog in a very big machine at Manchester United. There were far bigger cogs about, so I just rolled it on to a different part of the

1990: Paul Parker at Villa Park during Rangers' 2-2 draw

machine and let them make the match-winning pass. If I'd realised that a lot earlier I think I would have been the best right-back this country has ever produced."

Was losing the World Cup Semi-Final against Germany in Italia '90 the most disappointing thing to happen in your career or was the game your proudest achievement?

"To be honest I wasn't that disappointed - I'd achieved something I never thought I would.

I didn't think I'd get more than one game during the tournament because I had a hernia on the way and was getting pain-killing injections in my groin, plus I was recovering from a broken toe.

Before leaving for Italy all I was concerned about was whether I could train and run up and down the touch-line as sub and warm up - that was the limit of my hopes.

In the end I played six out of the seven games and I was just so happy to be in the Semi Final. When it went down to penalties I couldn't throw my boots away quick enough.

I couldn't have taken one with countless millions of people watching on the television all over the world, I tell you, it was never going to be me taking one of those spot kicks.

I didn't get upset or emotional although I suppose if we'd got to the Final we could have won it. The team got better as the tournament progressed and I think we really deserved to win against Germany.

But I've got a solid bronze medal and at this moment in time there are only twenty-two players who own winners medals in the country and only twenty-four with bronze medals - I'm happy to be one of that minority."

When you got home did you get much stick because of your deflection on 'that' German goal?

I still get stick today - there have been a couple of nasty incidents too. I was at a dinner where one of the speakers, who knew I was there, kept saying that 'Paul Parker cost us the World Cup'.

In the end I felt embarrassed for the guy because a lot of people knew me there and nobody laughed, he made an idiot of himself.

The worst thing about the night was when my missus went to the bar to get a pint of coke to throw over the bloke, luckily a mate's wife spotted her and calmly sat her down and stopped her from attacking him.

But there have been a lot of people who've shouted out snide remarks since, but I just look at them and laugh.

If I meant to do it, well, come and punch me on the nose right now, most people realise I did what I had to do, it was just a freak goal."

As a player you were always pretty calm and collected at QPR, apart from the time you kicked Gary Megson in the stomach!

"In fact I kneed him. It was a very tense game for some reason, I think it was because of all the speculation around Peter Reid moving to Manchester City. But the thing that made me snap more than anything was when Paul Lake broke Simon Barker's leg during the game.

I was really worried about a good mate being badly injured and it was playing on my mind as the game went on - I got the right hump. Then Gary Megson kept clipping my heels, over and over again until one time he caught me and we fell over together and I lost it completely. Something happened and I just laid into him. I knew what was coming and walked towards the tunnel before the referee had even got his card out.

But I'm not big enough to fight anyone really, I only did it because there were 14,000 fans on my side, ten other team mates and a referee to protect me.

It was just after that when I broke my toe and I almost missed out on the World Cup because of the suspension from that sending off. Bobby Robson had to fight my case with the authorities and I was eventually allowed to go."

I don't suppose there was much to consider when you were asked to join Manchester United was there?

"Well I turned down a move to Arsenal and an offer from Spurs, the team I support, to go to United. I made my mind up as soon as I arrived there for talks - it's the kind of place that a player falls in love with.

But even though I had a great time with United and grew up at Fulham from a young age, Rangers' results are still the ones that interest me the most. At the end of the day, Rangers was the club where I made my name, Rangers was the club where I earned my spurs as an International and Rangers allowed me to become a top class professional in Division One.

QPR and Jim Smith are the ones I owe everything to, they took a chance on me and I like to think that I didn't let them down.

I wish I'd left Fulham three years earlier, I wish I could have gone to QPR three years earlier and I wish I'd gone to Manchester United three years earlier."

Talking of Manchester United, can we talk about New Years Day 1992? QPR fans would gladly crow on about that forever.

"I was really up for that game, I had been looking forward to it for weeks. The match was live on ITV and the kick off had been changed to five o'clock, which for a player is absolutely awful. We had training in the morning, then came back and had a light lunch at one o'clock in the hotel, but that gave us no time to relax. Normally, for an evening kick-off, I'd sleep for three or four hours after lunch, then get up and have egg on toast or something, then play the game. But because of the kick-off time it meant our routine had been thrown out.

There were also a few changes to the side, which affected the game, the Boss tried to rotate things. He brought in Lee Sharpe who'd been out injured, left out Ryan Giggs and brought in Mickey Phelan in front of me instead of Andrei Kanchelskis.

QPR were up for it, they raised their game as I remember we always did when we played at Old Trafford. Andy Sinton had a good game that day, he knew how to play against me and I couldn't get anywhere near him. Andy didn't put himself in a position where he had to run me, he played against my weaknesses. Dennis Bailey scored a hat-trick and Rangers simply got what they deserved.

All the newspapers tried to make out that we'd been on the booze celebrating the boss' birthday on New Year's Eve - what a load of rubbish. That excuse takes too much away from QPR, we were battered from start to finish, it was as simple as that.

I remember walking off the pitch and hearing the QPR fans singing 'you should have stayed with the Rangers'."

Tony Ingham

1963: Tony Ingham [far left] and the Rangers squad at the White City stadium

**Date: Thursday 19th September, 2002
Venue: Tony's house, Stanmore
Era: 1950-1963 Appearances: 555 Goals: 3**

A book about Queen's Park Rangers wouldn't be complete without Tony Ingham's inclusion and this publication is no exception. Tony personifies everything good about football and possessed the kind of attributes that have largely evaporated over the years. His commitment and loyalty to Rangers were amazing and his staggering appearance record is unlikely ever to be broken.

Born in Harrogate in 1925, Ingham originally played for Leeds United before making the long move south to Queen's Park Rangers in 1950. Tony would make the left-back position his own for the next thirteen seasons and was a virtually ever-present for an eleven year period, a record he is extremely modest about. In fact Tony jokes about it, claiming his consistency was only due to the fact that he was too slow to get injured!

Following his retirement in 1963, Tony followed up his mammoth playing career with a further thirty-plus years service to QPR in various administrative capacities and was involved with corporate hospitality at the club until only recently. A total involvement spanning almost fifty years.

One thing you generally find with players of Tony's generation is that their thoughts on modern day football can be far from complimentary. Greedy players, too much money and faceless stadiums are common beliefs, but not for Tony. He still loves the game, in fact he thinks it's harder, faster and more pressurised than it was in his day and he doesn't begrudge his contemporaries a penny despite only earning a modest salary himself.

Tony watched QPR grow from humble beginnings in 1950 and he played through to Alec Stock's early sides. As a player he made a massive contribution to the start of Rangers' rise through the leagues and as a loyal club servant he had the pleasure of being able to see those early foundations built upon in the best possible way by the players that followed him.

It was a huge honour to spend an evening with Tony at his home and I must admit to being like a kid in a sweet shop when his daughter arrived laden with her father's numerous football scrap-books and photo albums. Ingham's family have kept a meticulous record of his football career which includes cuttings as far back as his Harrogate school-boy team, his first professional contract with Leeds United and hundreds of newspaper reports from his endeavours for Queen's Park Rangers.

Witnessing Tony's face light up as he flicked through the pages himself for the first time in years is a memory that will always stay with me.

You moved to Rangers in 1950, established yourself in the first two seasons then barely missed a match for ten solid seasons. That is a fantastic level of consistency, so how do you react when you hear of players today like Patrick Vieira getting tired five games into a season?

"Oh it's a completely different game now, it's so much faster and the players are under a lot more pressures than they were in my time. It's win at all costs now and the tackles are harder, their bodies take more of a pounding today because there's so much more at stake in the games they play at the top level."

Moving from Leeds to London at the time must have involved quite some upheaval, did you settle in to London life easily?

"Well it's funny really because I told my wife that we'd only come down for a year or two, but as you can see I stayed down here a lot longer! We moved into a flat in Kenton when I first arrived, a club place that cost fifty shillings a week, but I settled in fairly quickly I think."

What was training like in the fifties and how did methods change while you were at the club?

"Well, it wasn't really training as such, not anything like the QPR players have now. We used to run from morning 'till night clock-wise around the pitch, then we'd come in the next day and do the same thing in reverse.

[Laughs] That was the training, we never saw a ball apart from pre-season and match days. Later on, nearer the end of my playing career at QPR, things had changed and there was more of an emphasis on tactics and ball work, but in the early days it was very, very different."

You only played under three managers during your time at QPR; Dave Mangnall, Jack Taylor and Alec Stock. How did they compare?

"I thought Alec was the best by a long way, he knew what he wanted and knew what to say in the dressing room to get the most out of you on the pitch. Mangnall and Taylor were nice chaps but they weren't as knowledge-able I didn't think."

Alec Stock obviously put a great side together at QPR which started to blossom in the late 1960s. You'd finished playing by that stage and missed out on that success, but you must have seen the start of Stock's famous side. Was that an exciting time to be at QPR, could you see that the club were moving forward?

"Yes you could, he started to bring in some great players and he moulded them into a fantastic football team.

Marshy was starting to come good by then and of course would go on to be a great player for QPR."

You played in Rangers' record league victory, our 9-2 win against Tranmere, do you remember that day?
"I do, I must admit that the games start to get a bit fuzzy, but I remember it was a fantastic game to play in. I gave their second goal away but the manager didn't seem too bothered about it though. But if I hadn't there would have only been ten goals in the game!"

Looking back, are there any games that stand out in your memory from that era?
"I clearly remember playing against Tom Finney in a league game once, he was a great player. I remember playing against Stanley Matthews in a testimonial game, I had to mark him too!
Even though it wasn't a really competitive game, he was a real handful, mind you, he only agreed to play in the first place on the condition that no one was allowed to tackle him. That didn't make it any easier though!
I can't remember whose testimonial it was, we had a lot of them back then, but they meant something and the players genuinely needed them. I had two myself in my time at QPR."

Everyone at QPR always talks about Bowles and Marsh, but another forward that often gets overlooked and who doesn't get the recognition they probably should is Brian Bedford. He scored 180 goals in 284 games for Rangers which is an amazing record isn't it?
"Yes, Brian was a real battler and was the sort of player who could score goals with his back-side if he had to. If you had a go at him on the pitch he'd shout back at you, 'I'm trying, I'm trying...' and the thing is, he really was. He was a good lad was Brian, a good striker. He was good in the air, he used to get in the box, he was a brave player too.
We didn't pay much for him as I remember [£750 from Bournemouth], so he was quite a bargain. After I finished playing there was another lad who didn't get the credit he deserved - Les Allen. In my eyes Les made Rodney Marsh.
But as you go back in time players get forgotten. The Morgan twins, Ian and Roger, they did a great job for Rangers too and Mike Ferguson, he was some player."

Do you remember your goals for QPR, all three of them?
"[Laughs] I only remember one goal, but that was a hard one to forget really - I hit it from the half-way line.

Tony Ingham leap-frogs Arthur Longbottom during training

1952: Tony Ingham and Rangers 'keeper Harry Brown watch a shot go just wide

I remember I went in for a 50-50 with this guy who was coming in for a tackle, anyway I just whacked it as hard as I could just before the half-way line and the 'keeper was off his line and it sailed over his head and into the net.

It was a great goal to score and I'll never forget that one. David Beckham does that and they say he's a genius!

I think somebody else tried to claim that one and they tried to take it off me, but I'll always see it as my goal."

You got sent off in controversial circumstances didn't you?

"I did yes, I threw the ball at the opposing manager! We were playing Shrewsbury and I threw the ball back to their bench then I looked round and saw their manager, Harry Potts, lying on the floor spark out!

The referee didn't see it but their players rushed round him and said "he hit him ref, he hit him" so he sent me off on their word.

I've had a few drinks with that referee since at functions and he still remembers the game. I was cleared by the FA in the end though."

You played your last season with QPR away from Loftus Road - at the old White City Stadium. What was it like playing there?

"I didn't like it at the White City, there was no atmosphere what-so-ever as the crowd was too far away from you. There was a running track around the edge of the pitch and it seemed a long way away from the fans.

I don't know whether that had an effect on the players or not, it's hard to say, but it couldn't have helped us. I would have much rather had my last season at the club at Loftus Road though."

Why did you stop playing when you did?

"I'd had enough really [laughs]. You've got to remember we didn't have long contract deals then, we only signed year to year. You had to play to get your wages and the maximum wage was still in place. I enjoyed my time though and I wouldn't change it for anything."

You stayed at the club for years after you finished playing, it must've been nice to remain connected?

"Definitely, but it wasn't the same. You miss playing, especially the banter and camaraderie in the dressing room. In saying that, though, it was lovely to stay within the club and I thoroughly enjoyed it.

It was great interacting with all the managers and players through the years. Terry Venables used to give me some stick from time to time and we used to tease each other about our football careers. I used to say to him 'how many games did you play for QPR?' and he'd turn round and say 'yeah,

QUEEN'S PARK RANGERS SUPPORTER'S CLUB

Y INGHAM TESTIMONIAL MATCH

QUEENS PARK RANGERS

v

INTERNATIONAL XI

WEDNESDAY 3rd MAY Kick-off 7.30

OFFICIAL PROGRAMME   6d.

2002: Tony proudly displays his testimonial programme

yeah Tony, get your England caps out!' He was a great character to have around the club and I really enjoyed working with him at QPR."

Do you still enjoy watching football today? Is it the same game you played or has some of the sport been removed?

"I still enjoy it, yes. If there's a match on the TV I'll always watch it. But even with all the money and pressure in today's game, once that whistle goes it's still the same game.

The players are paid more these days but I don't begrudge them that, good luck to them. People say they are overpaid but I don't think so."

You're the record appearance holder at QPR, a record that will probably never be beaten. That's some achievement isn't it?

"Records are made to be beaten so you never know. It's something I'm very proud of though, we played a lot more games in those days so that helped me cram so many games into my career.

People say that I barely missed a game in ten years, but that was only because I was too slow to get injured!"

1967: Lazarus battles for the ball against Norwich City

Mark Lazarus

Date: Friday 8th November, 2002
Venue: Mark's house, Romford, Essex
Era: 1960-1967 Appearances: 233 Goals: 84

For a man who by his own admission had little more than a passing interest in the game of football, Mark Lazarus still managed to write himself into Queen's Park Rangers folklore. Mark achieved many notable milestones in his seventeen year career, including becoming the most transferred player in QPR's history and being the only footballer to win four promotions in successive seasons. For Rangers fans however, he will be eternally remembered for one thing, and that, of course, is scoring the winning goal in the 1967 League Cup Final which secured QPR's first (and only) cup victory.

We all know the tale, Third Division Rangers were two-nil down against First Division West Brom at half time, then came out to win the game three-two. But however glorious that moment was for the club, Lazarus had a far greater input into Queen's Park Rangers' illustrious history than just that strike. He was one of the best wingers to ever turn out for the club and enjoyed so much success during the club's first golden age. He rightly points out that he and his sixties team-mates laid the foundations which enabled QPR to build upon. If it wasn't for them and all the glory, who knows what sort of club we would have become, perhaps without that team later success would never have happened.

He mentions the money he made Rangers in his three transfers from Loftus Road, but aside from that, he played a key part in both of our promotion winning seasons, from the Third Division to Second in 1967 and from the Second to First the following year.

Mark played for Rangers in three separate spells, he also featured for Brentford, Leyton Orient (twice), Wolves and Crystal Palace. Remarkably, despite all the moves, he still managed to play in 233 games for QPR and he makes it clear that he never asked to leave Rangers, not once.

Meeting Mark was an excellent experience, it's clear for someone who takes little interest in today's game that his time in football and at QPR was very, very special to him. One thing I truly hope is that his words on paper don't sound arrogant because he certainly did not come across that way in person. He is simply (and rightly) proud of his and his team's achievements and obviously feels credit should be given where credit is due. By all means remember THAT goal but never forget the rest of this remarkable man's contributions.

After football Lazarus built up a large removals business in Romford and still runs a popular Steam Bath and Spa in Canning Town.

You came from a family of boxers, when you were growing up did that seem a more natural career for you?

"Yes, in actual fact I didn't see anything other than fighting as a career. I was going to box professionally, my brothers boxed and fighting was the only sport that was talked about in our house.

I was playing for Orient at the time and it was only because they asked me to turn pro that really changed things, as once I'd signed they wouldn't allow me to box any more - so that put an end to that. But I've always kept up my interest in boxing, it was my first love. In fact I didn't really know anything about football when I turned pro in 1957. I was boxing as an amateur and was quite a useful fighter - I'd never been beaten.

Three months after turning pro I had to do my national service in the Army and when I came out Les Gorre, who had replaced Alec Stock as Orient manager, told me he felt there wasn't much of a future for me in football.

Alec had moved on to QPR but when he knew I was out of the Army he came in for me. When Gorre told me that Rangers wanted me, I thought he meant Glasgow Rangers – that's how little I knew about football!

I remember when Alec used to run through the other side's players in team talks, telling me who to mark and that, I didn't know who any of them were! As I say, football in my life was a secondary sport, but I ended up having seventeen years in the game and I still don't know anything about it. I don't watch football and I don't take any interest in it to this day - football was just a job.

Don't get me wrong, I really, really enjoyed my time in the game, but I have to be really forced to go and watch a game now. I keep an eye on the results in the 'papers but that's as far as it goes. I don't think I've been back to QPR since I left."

How would you describe yourself as a player?

"I didn't have any magic as a player, but there was no one who played football with a bigger heart than me. I was two footed and I didn't know which one was best. I scored goals, I ran at people and I brought a bit of excitement to a game. When I got the ball the crowd would rise. I wasn't afraid to go in where it hurts, if people kicked me I kicked them back.

The supposed modern day hard men, Robbie Savage and Vinny Jones, they aren't fit to lace my boots. They're not hard men. Don Megson [father of Gary], he was a hard man, they used to keep him caged up during the week and tease him with a football then let him loose on a Saturday!"

Who were your good mates at QPR?

"Rodney Marsh was a very good friend of mine, I got on very well with him. He thinks quite highly of me and so he should. This might sound boastful to you but Rodney Marsh was an ordinary player when he came to QPR - Fulham didn't want him and they weren't a particularly good side. He had skill, but skill can be found in a lot of players that go nowhere.

The likes of myself and Les Allen did him the biggest favour he ever had in the game. Les used to create a lot of space and I'd put the ball in for Rodney to score. He netted forty-four goals in one season and you could count on one hand how many of them were self made.

Rodney picked a Dream XI for a newspaper once that included George Best, Bobby Moore, Jimmy Greaves, Pele, Johan Cruyff and me! Either he's taking the piss or he actually thinks that highly of me."

You had seven clubs between 1960 and 1970, what made you keep moving around?

"Well I've explained the first move to QPR, going back with Alec Stock was the deciding factor in that. But six months later Wolves came in for me, which was astounding. It would be like Manchester United coming in for you today – you go! Wolves' manager at the time, Stan Cullis, told me that if I turned him down he was going to go and sign Mike Summerbee. I couldn't believe he would pick me over Mike. I think the fee was £27,000, which at the time was a lot of money for QPR, so I went.

Unfortunately I made the wrong decision and Wolves became the only club I ever asked to leave. Stan Cullis was a sergeant major type and talked to people like shit, but I used to answer him back and stick up for other players when he started on them. So we were never going to get along and QPR ended up buying me back, which was perfect for me as I'd never really left them. I was still training at QPR during the week and travelling up to Wolverhampton on Friday for the match the next day, then back down to train at QPR on the Monday. I wish I'd never moved to Wolves.

I later found out that I could have gone to Tottenham or West Ham, which probably would have suited me better, but Alec Stock didn't let on that they were interested in me because they both offered less money.

I had a good time at QPR again, then Brentford came in for me. They were a good side in those days and they wanted to swap me for George McLeod and £8,000. That was a another good deal for QPR so I was on my way once more. I had a terrific time at Brentford, enjoyed my football and had a good relationship with the fans, then, after about two seasons, Alec Stock brought me back to QPR again!

He was trying to build a good side and wanted me in it, so I went back. That was a great period obviously, that's when we had all the success, but one day I went into work and found out that Crystal Palace wanted me and Rangers were prepared to let me leave again.

THE FOOTBALL LEAGUE

CUP FINAL

QUEEN'S PARK RANGERS
VERSUS
WEST BROMWICH ALBION
(HOLDERS)

SATURDAY MARCH 4th. 1967

Lazarus
REMOVALS

2002: Lazarus poses with the 1967 League Cup Final programme

1967: Rangers fans invade the pitch to celebrate the sides League Cup Semi-Final win

Ian Morgan was coming through at QPR and had been substitute for practically every game. I think QPR thought they had my position well covered and I was starting to get on a bit, so I was off again!

I think QPR made about £50,000 profit on me moving backwards and forwards, so they did well out of me.

I had a great time at Palace, we got promoted, the crowd were brilliant to me and I had great success. We got to the First Division but I was starting to have problems with the coach George Petchey. I couldn't stand the man and he didn't like me - actually he didn't like anyone. I used to offer him outside three times a day!

Then Jimmy Bloomfield, an old team mate of mine at Brentford, had taken over as manager at Leyton Orient. He begged me to go back there, so that's what I did. In doing so I got promoted again, which was my fourth season in a row, which is still a record to this day. But in all the moves I had, I only ever asked to leave one club - Wolves."

How did you enjoy playing under Alec Stock?

"I hold him in such high esteem, I really do. Whilst he didn't have a great football brain he was a tremendous influence on me as player - he was an amazing motivator. Mind you, we had some terrible rows - sometimes he'd literally slap me around at half time! The next day he'd put his arm round me and ask how I was. If you had any problems or worries at home you could go to Alec and he'd sort it.

All he ever used to shout from the dug out was 'kick it, kick it, kick it' but you would never walk into Alec Stock's dressing room and wonder who was the boss - you knew. He just had that sort of great presence."

What did Alec say to the players at half time during the League Cup Final after QPR went in 2-0 down to West Bromwich Albion?

"Well you have to remember we were a Third Division side playing at Wembley against a First Division side, so it was a bit different. Mind you when I think back we were always losing at half time during that cup run, we were a second half side.

All Alec said to us was 'go out and enjoy yourselves'. It would have spoilt the day if he had done his nut. He said 'we're better than this, just go out and show the crowd what you can do', which is what we did."

What are your memories of that day?

"I know I got the winning goal in the game, but one thing that disappoints me about that day is that I could have had a hat-trick. I hit the post and I had a volley cleared off the line as well. It was a wonderful day, but beating Birmingham to get to Wembley was more exciting I thought.

We were one-nil down at half time in the first leg which wasn't a disaster because we knew we'd beat them at Loftus Road. I don't even think today's Manchester United side would have beaten us at Loftus Road back then!

I remember the ride from our hotel to Wembley Stadium, the streets were lined with QPR fans before the game, thousands and thousands of them - it was like a procession by the Royal Family.

All the way down Westbourne Park and down the Marylebone Road, it was amazing. Houses were covered in blue and white and some people had even painted their cars in the hoops!

All my family were there supporting me at the match too - they used to follow me everywhere. It was lovely day, great memories and no one can ever take them away from me."

Which did you enjoy more, the Cup win or the League Championship?
"Let me put it like this, some people go into work and there are people they don't like or don't get on with. I'm not lying when I say this, but everybody got on so well at QPR that we couldn't get into work quick enough, we even wanted to go in on our days off!

Myself, Mickey Leach and Roger Morgan all used to get the Central Line into Loftus Road and we'd have a great laugh all the way there and all the way back - it was such a good club at that time. Success helped, but there was so much more to it than that. That season wasn't just about winning the League and The Cup, it was the atmosphere at QPR that made the place so special - I never had another club like it.

We won the league with about seven games to go, but if I had to make a choice and I could only win one thing that year, I would take the League Championship as that was more important to the club. But I couldn't say which I enjoyed more."

Were you ever tempted to stay in the game in a coaching role?
"The closest I ever got to coaching was during one pre-season. This fifteen year old kid had come down to train with us and the scout Derek Healey wanted to have a good look at him, so the kid was paired off with me.

I told him to move twenty yards away, and that I was going to chip the ball to his feet. He was then supposed to chip it back. So I chipped it over to him, he tried to trap it but the ball ran up his legs and away from him, so he ran off to get the ball. Then he chipped it to me and it ended up miles away. We did this a few times and the same thing happened each time - he just couldn't trap the ball.

Jimmy Andrews, the coach, came over and asked me afterwards how it had gone, I said 'he was fucking useless'. That kid was Frank Sibley [165 games for QPR] so that shows what I know!"

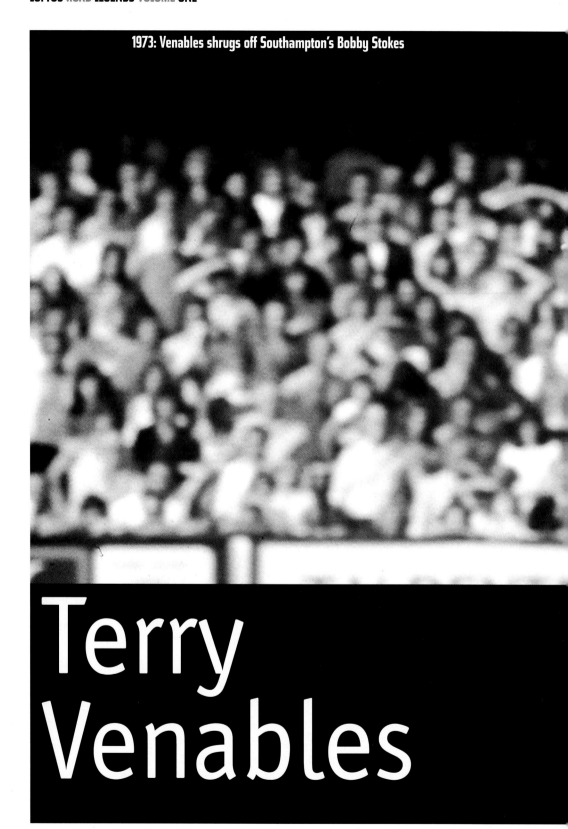

1973: Venables shrugs off Southampton's Bobby Stokes

Terry Venables

Date: Tuesday 1st October, 2002
Venue: Leeds United's Training Ground
Era: 1969-1974 Appearances: 205 Goals: 22

After serving his football apprenticeship and establishing a name for himself down the road at Stamford Bridge, Terry Venables joined QPR from Tottenham Hotspur in the Summer of 1969 following Rangers' brief flirtation with the top flight. He would become part of the back-bone of the midfield for five seasons and helped the club back to Division One in 1973. Terry then moved to Crystal Palace where his coaching career began under the colourful Malcolm Allison.

Not only did Terry play a vital role in changing the image of the football club on the pitch, his well publicised off the field antics were portrayed in the press in a glamourous light and along with the likes of David Webb and Rodney Marsh, Rangers became show-biz.

One of the things that amazed me while interviewing players for this book, was the genuine enthusiasm they all still have for Queen's Park Rangers and the sheer delight with which they reminisce about their days spent at Loftus Road.

But for a man who has managed top clubs in England and Spain, taken charge of his country and brought football "home", fought several personal battles and is now trying to turn around the fortunes of Leeds United, his memory of those five years at QPR are more vivid and fresh than I could have dreamed of. A genuine enthusiasm about Rangers is still very much alive and well within Terry.

His passion for the club is undoubted, every story was recounted with a cheeky smile and although you get the impression there was much more that couldn't be said, I don't think I will laugh as much in an hour for a very long time. You can see why players respond so well to Venables the manager, he has an infectious charm.

Meeting Terry Venables was always a dream of mine and therefore one of the few interviews I was a little nervous about - Terry put me at ease immediately though. Maybe I look at things through blue and white tinted spectacles, but after talking to Venables, I felt like he had a soft spot for QPR like no other club he has been involved with.

It's clear he loved every minute of his time as a player and manager, just as we loved having him - Terry even talked about getting a season ticket at QPR when he retires! But after seeing the spark in his eye, fresh from taking morning training with the Leeds players, I think that retirement could still be a long way off.

You signed from Tottenham in 1969 after a successful career at both White Hart Lane and Chelsea. Why did you choose QPR at that stage?

"Well, I had a terrific time at Chelsea, I was in the side at seventeen, Captain at nineteen and it was all happening for me. I played for England at twenty-one and then Tommy Docherty took over as Manager and there were a lot of changes.

I dictated things at Chelsea as a youngster, all the play used to go through me, but The Doc said it wasn't good to just go through one player, which was true. So he tried different methods which worked quite well. Then I went to Tottenham who were a very, very good side - they'd done the double in 1961 and were still a cracking team.

Alan Mullery had come in after Danny Blanchflower had retired, then I arrived. I took a different role because I couldn't demand the ball as much - Spurs was full of players better than I was. But I decided it was good for me to be more of a team player.

I don't think we were ever out of the top three while I was at White Hart Lane and we won the Cup, but I didn't play as well as I had done at Chelsea. I should have just been myself, I should have said 'this is me, if you like it you like it, if you don't, you don't'. For a confident player I was a bit nervous at Spurs, but I shouldn't have been. But things at Tottenham weren't as good as I would have liked. Then the chance of moving to QPR came along, so I thought I'd go down a division to find out if a change of club would help me regain my form.

I felt at home straight away at QPR, I thought it was great and I had a really good time there as a footballer. Funnily enough, although I was in the Second Division, England manager Alf Ramsey had started to talk about me again.

I thought that stage in my career was great for me, possibly almost as good as at Chelsea - especially the way I slotted in playing with Rodney [Marsh] and Barry Bridges who'd been with me at Stamford Bridge. It was great to be able to find myself again and I had a wonderful time at QPR."

Your £70,000 transfer fee was a record for QPR at the time, did that add any pressure to your move?

"No, not really. I went to Tottenham for £80,000 three years earlier, which was quite a big fee.

It was funny, I'd played against QPR when I was at Tottenham and Bobby Keetch, who was a very good friend of mine, was a very hard player back then. He was really tough and he'd go for you. Anyway, during the game there was no doubt that he was going to 'do' me, the ball came to me and I could see him coming towards me - so I just put my foot high. I didn't move, I just waited for him to hit me. I kept my foot there and he went straight through it and the stretcher had to be brought on for him. He was calling me everything under the sun.

After the game I went in to see how he was, but before I went into the dressing room I could hear all the swearing from inside, so I knocked on the door, opened it and saw Jim Gregory talking to him. So I said, 'Bob, are you okay?'... Then he went in to one... He shouted, 'Okay? Am I okay? Does it look like I'm 'effing okay? Look at my bloody leg!' I said, 'yeah, okay Bob, I'll speak to you later, sorry about that...' Then he just went in to one again. So I said, 'look, I can see it's not a good time...', and all the other players were laughing, so I walked away.

It was only a little while after that I signed for QPR and I remember Jim Gregory saying to me that Keetchy had told him that he had to sign me because of my front - [laughs] putting him on a stretcher then coming in to see if he was alright."

Didn't Rodney Marsh claim that he played a big part in getting Jim Gregory to sign you from Spurs?

"[Laughs] Rodney Marsh claims everything. What he claims and what is reality are two very strange bed partners I think."

Your arrival saw the start of QPR's climb and our subsequent challenge for the First Division title, could you see that potential slowly building?

"Yeah, I thought we looked a strong side. We did well in the Cup too when I arrived, until we played the eventual winners Chelsea - they really beat us up [QPR lost 4-2 in the 6th round at Loftus Road].

But QPR had a really good side, we got promoted three seasons later. Then we added players like Webby [David Webb] and Frank McLintock.

Funny enough I nearly went back to play for QPR, before Dave Sexton went in for Don Masson. He enquired about me and I spoke to him, but it just didn't go ahead, I don't know what happened, whether he couldn't sign me or whether he preferred Masson, I'm not quite sure. I got on really well with Dave - we were together at Chelsea."

You were signed by Les Allen, who was then replaced by Gordon Jago. How would you compare the two?

"They were both decent people, I enjoyed it under both managers. I remember before one match Gordon Jago came in to the dressing room, which was a tough old place at the time. We had Rodney Marsh, Mike Ferguson, Bridges, Allan Harris - a hefty school of characters.

Anyway, Jago went into this rousing pre-match speech about what we had to do during the game... 'I want this and I want that, I expect that...'

it was a very, very good speech. [Laughs] Then Marshy stood up at the end and said, 'Gordon, we're all with you 40%'.

I was Captain at the time and Gordon started asking me to go out and warm the players up before training. It started off just being once or twice, when he said he was busy in the office, but then it became an every day occurrence. Eventually I turned round and said to him, 'Gordon don't you think it's about time you got someone in', because it was happening every day. He said 'no, no, don't worry, it's alright... by the way, have you got £5 I can borrow?' I replied, 'sure, no problem', and I gave him the five quid and he walked away.

Anyway, about four weeks went by and I hadn't seen the return of my fiver, then before another game he went into another one of his rousing speeches... 'I won't be happy until every player here is a top man, I want every one of you to have a Rolls Royce...' I couldn't resist it, I just piped up 'never mind the Rolls Royce Gordon, where's my bloody fiver?'"

Did you ever get it back?
"No, I didn't actually, but it was well worth it for the joke!"

You mentioned that Jago tricked you in to taking a lot of coaching, but was it always clear to you that this is where your future in football would be?
"Well I took my coaching badge when I was in my very early twenties in fact - I always enjoyed it. If you get ninety-five or more out of a hundred you got a distinction, which I'd got at a young age.

I was really pleased by that as I was a bit nervous taking it with a lot of older people around and my involvement in coaching eventually meant that when I retired I didn't miss playing that much. I had arthritis in my ankle and Malcolm Allison offered me a chance at Crystal Palace.

I remember going to a party one New Year's Eve at a friend's house and Frank McLintock and Bobby Moore were there. Our wives were on one side of the room and us three were wedged in the corner, as you do. I told them that I was going to stop playing and take up coaching full time - they said I was mad. I said to them that if I missed the actual playing, I could take part in the five-a-sides but they thought they'd miss actually playing in front of crowds.

I knew they both wanted to become coaches eventually too, which they did, but I told them that if I started earlier I'd be up and running a lot sooner and would have a head start. I was really into it - I really wanted to do it. Eventually, when it came round to them trying to find coaching jobs after they'd retired they struggled to find clubs and I helped both with their first coaching roles - Bobby at Crystal Palace and Frank at QPR."

Terry Venables celebrates scoring a goal at Loftus Road

During the course of conducting the interviews for this book I've heard Jim Gregory described as everything from 'Mr. QPR' to 'an arsehole', whereabouts in that scale did he fit in your view?

"[Laughs] Well, Jim was a tough businessman, you've only got to remember what Loftus Road was like when I was a player, it was just a tin shed of a ground.

When I joined, the dressing rooms were on the other side of the ground to where they are now and the roof slanted so if you were at that end of the room you had to duck while you were getting changed. It was so tight in there it was amazing. But at the end of the day, the history that you are capturing by speaking to the players for your book wouldn't be the same if it wasn't for Jim Gregory.

He was tough, he was over-hard, he was amusing and every post was a winning post with Jim. But he used to say the same about me and more than likely that's why we got on. I got on well with him as a player and as a manager.

I used to go over and see him a couple of times a week when I was manager and talk football with him, it was a joy, not a hardship, as he was really good on his football. I would see him once, often twice a week after training and we would talk sometimes until half past eight at night. But he *was* QPR really and a hard act to follow."

Rodney Marsh describes players like you, himself, Barry Bridges, Keith Sanderson, Alan Harris etc., as 'The Rangers Rat Pack' and talks of you all drinking your way around West London. Is that how it was?

"Well, I don't think it was that bad. If we did have a night out, we'd have a good'un, but it wasn't every night or anything like that. But we certainly enjoyed each other's company.

Terry Mancini was another one who had a great personality. We would have a couple of beers after training sometimes, but I don't recall 'drinking from Ruislip up to Town' as Rodney mentions. [Laughs] I'm never sure how good Rodney's memory is.

There was a pub called The Feathers we used a lot, by the Chiswick roundabout, just down the road from where Gerry Francis used to live. We'd meet up there and go out for the evening. But it was a very different way of life when we were playing to what it is like now.

I say to the players at Leeds that although we used to enjoy ourselves more socially back then, we didn't have the big money they enjoy. It was good money, but it wasn't that far away from a lot of people who were doing well in life, the money certainly wasn't huge like it is now.

The trouble is that you can go out drinking on a Thursday night and still play well on Saturday, but later in life it catches up with you I think. But

2002: Terry ponders a question at Leeds United's training ground

in my day players would retire about the age of thirty-two, today there's more and more players continuing at the top level until thirty-six. If you can get another five years earning two million pounds per season by keeping in good condition it's obviously a very worthwhile exercise."

You were the penalty taker at QPR and scored quite a few while you were at the club.

"[Laughs] Well you would do if you had Rodney in the team wouldn't you? When I arrived I think I took about ten penalties in a fairly short space of time and Rodney got them all. It was embarrassing [laughs], he had this knack of kicking himself and going up in the air. He used to shout 'penalty!' and I used to think 'oh no, not another one'.

It was quite ironic, because Gerry Francis and Rodney were always having a go at each other and there was certainly a lot of feeling between the two of them.

Anyway, we went up to play Manchester City after Rodney had moved up there and Gerry and I were talking about his knack of winning penalties on the way up to the game. During the match Rodney went to shoot and Gerry dived in to stop him, Marsh hit his leg and went up in the air... Penalty! Gerry Francis couldn't believe it, he couldn't believe he'd fallen for it."

Apart from penalties, what are your favourite goals from open play?

"I remember we used to do this free-kick routine where we used to lift the ball straight over the wall and Gerry used to volley it in the net, they were always good. But you could get away with a lot more then because you weren't on telly every game and there weren't any action replays showing every single incident.

I remember a game where we thrashed Birmingham City 5-2, Rodney scored a hat trick but I also got one. Birmingham had Mike Kelly, who had been with us at Rangers and he was always threatening Rodney. Kelly was chasing him all over the pitch trying to catch him like he used to do in training at QPR, that was very funny."

If you had the chance to buy Stan Bowles or Rodney Marsh in their prime for Leeds, who would you pick?

"They were very different I think - Rodney was always very flamboyant and really wanted to please the crowd. I don't see anything wrong with that, because he was effective as well as skillful and used to score a lot of goals while entertaining the supporters. Whereas Stan was hugely talented too, but very businesslike - he wanted to win.

People may not have realised it, but he had this uncanny ability to know what to do with the ball and when. The first day that Stan arrived in training we played an eight-a-side game and from that first day it looked as though Stan and Gerry Francis had been playing together forever, the one-two's and movement were amazing.

Stan was serious about his football, although he wasn't serious about himself and his life. But he wanted to win and he did things well. I had a lot of time for Stan, I thought he was a wonderful player."

You left QPR the season before Rangers finished second, do you regret not being around for that?

"Yeah, but I was nearing the end of my career. In my life I've been fortunate with timing and unfortunate with timing - more often than not it's just luck where you land and at what moment.

It's like here at Leeds now, they've spent £200 million in the past few years and I arrive when they're saving up [laughs]. So you've got to have a bit of good fortune, I went to Barcelona at the right time so things often even themselves out.

Sometimes you can be very fortunate, in other cases you can be very unlucky and on other occasions you need more time and don't get it."

When the call came from Jim Gregory to manage Rangers, was it too good an opportunity to turn down?

"Funny enough Jim tried to get me to manage QPR just after I'd signed for Crystal Palace in 1974. I'd only been gone a few weeks. Jim spoke to Malcolm Allison about offering me the manager's job after Gordon Jago left Rangers and they'd had a meeting about it - but for some reason it didn't go through. [Laughs] He must have missed our chats.

But eventually, after I'd been manager at Palace for a few years he came in for me again. We'd got Palace promoted from the Third Division to the Second, won the Second Division Championship, then gone up to the First Division. But we'd had a bad start in Division One and were struggling a bit.

Jim was straight in and he offered Palace £100,000 for me. I remember Palace's Chairman, Raymond Bloye, came to me and said 'what do you want to do?' I replied, 'no, what do you want to do? If you take the money I'll go, if you don't, I'll stay.'

I think it was very tempting for Palace at the time and after about twelve games we were low down in the table, so they took the money. That really upset me, it was my first manager's job and we'd done really well taking them from the bottom of Division Three all the way to Division One.

QPR were near the bottom when I arrived and we were able to get them up to safety. The next year we got to the Cup Final against Spurs, then the following season we won the Second Division Championship."

What was your relationship like with Dave Sexton?

"We had a very happy relationship. I'd played for him at Chelsea and we worked together as coaches with England at under-21 level.

It never seems to get a mention but in 1982 we won the European Championship against Germany when Pierre Littbarski was playing for them. We beat them over two legs, up at Sheffield United then over in Germany - we won that together with him as the manager and me as the coach."

Looking at QPR's position now and the situation the club has faced in recent seasons, do you feel any emotion towards the club's plight?

"Well I still live at Brook Green so I know a lot of QPR supporters. In fact I was talking to one the other day who was saying he's not enjoyed the last five or six years, so it's nice that they're starting to do well again at the moment and getting the fans feeling good about things again. I know they obviously want to do better, but the club holds fantastic memories for me, both as a player and a manager.

Getting Rangers to the Cup Final and taking Tottenham to two games was terrific I thought, and the first year back in Division One we qualified for Europe. Then I went to Barcelona.

[Laughs] When I retire from football I think I'll get a season ticket at Rangers and walk down there and enjoy the football in my old age."

1982: Gary Waddock during the FA Cup Final

Gary Waddock

Date: Thursday 10th October, 2002
Venue: QPR Training Ground, Acton
Era: 1979-1992 Appearances: 227 Goals: 10

I was always impressed by Gary Waddock as a player. People may describe him as being a gritty, no-nonsense midfielder, but that would not do full justice to a very talented player and what I learnt from meeting him is that he is as impressive a man as he was a footballer. Waddock's traumatic injury problems show that he is as strong mentally as his playing style proved he was physically.

Gary has been through some very hard times in his career, he has hit rock bottom and battled his way back to the very top. When every doctor worth his salt told Waddock his football career was over, he refused to accept their decisions and fought back through the pain barrier to prove them all wrong. Not only did Gary return to the professional game, playing in both Belgium and England, but his remarkable recovery even saw him win further caps for the Irish Republic. As Gary justifiably points out, "that's not bad for someone with a dodgy knee!"

The ups and downs of Gary Waddock's life make for fascinating reading, signed as an apprentice in 1979, making his debut the same year aged just seventeen, he would go on to become a regular in the side for five seasons. Gary enjoyed FA Cup Finals, a promotion to the top flight and is one of very few QPR players to perform in European competition. Then in 1986, having achieved so much, it seemed that a blossoming career was about to be snatched away due to a bad knee injury that threatened his livelihood.

Many would have given up but Gary is made of stronger stuff, he bravely battled on, every knock back just seemed to inspire him and after six years of hell, he would return to QPR and cap a glorious and truly remarkable comeback.

I don't know if Gary would agree, but I find it a relief that he was able to enjoy success early on in his career before the injury struck. The FA Cup Finals against Tottenham, although ultimately unsuccessful, were a fantastic achievement for the then Second Division side and the promotion season that followed under Terry Venables provided Rangers fans with some of their most halcyon days. I would hate to think that a player of Waddock's ability were to miss out on memories such as these due to one stroke of bad luck.

Gary often features in fans all time QPR XI's, which is quite a testament for someone whose Rangers career was effectively over at only twenty-four years of age.

You signed for QPR as an apprentice and now you are in charge of that area of the club, do you wish you'd grown up in the sort of environment you're now working in?

"[Laughs] That's a good question. I came to the club as a young lad of twelve or thirteen and there were good coaches around at the time, people like Theo Foley. He was an excellent coach and Theo really helped me in those early days, seeing me through the youth team, the reserves, then into the first team.

I'd like to think I'm doing an OK job here, I try to put on training sessions that not only improve the players but also sessions that I would have enjoyed being a part of myself. I've had no complaints as yet! "

How would you compare the training the young players get at Queen's Park Rangers today to what you had?

"Well times have changed, the game's got a lot quicker, people are looking for more mobile, athletic players these days. Back when I started they were always looking for the flair player but you don't see as many of them these days. There's a lot more work being put into weights, agility work etc.., which is a part of their weekly training schedule. I can't ever remember doing anything like that.

Basically they're athletes these days, even the food they eat is gauged and monitored in the build up to a game. When I was playing you'd just have steak and chips, but that's totally out of the question now.

Here we're trying to educate the boys to start eating properly from the age of fourteen, because if they get into good habits now they'll take it through the rest of their careers.

If they do, then it will extend their careers, people are already playing well into their thirties now. It's changed totally in the last fifteen years and what I'll find interesting is how things move in the next fifteen years."

You made your debut at just seventeen, what do you remember about the occasion?

"My full league debut was against Charlton, the manager was Tommy Docherty at the time - he was a fantastic character.

I turned up at the ground and found out I was in the squad - I only had an hour to take it all in. I think Tommy handled that the right way, if he'd told me on the Friday I wouldn't have been able to sleep. I'll never forget it though, we won four-nil. Tommy told me how well I'd played but left me out for the next game! I was gutted.

Again, he did the right thing. When the next game came around he pulled me aside and said I wasn't playing and explained why. I was devastated but it gave me a taste and I wanted it even more then."

Tommy Docherty left shortly afterwards and was replaced by Terry Venables. What impact did his departure have on you?

"Looking back now it was unsettling. You never know when a new manager comes in if you'll be playing or not, but I was fortunate to be already training with the first team so I had the chance to impress the new boss from day one. I consider myself fortunate to have played under Tommy Docherty though, I certainly learned a lot from him."

Terry Venables was almost as colourful a character as Tommy Docherty, but how did they compare as managers?

"Well it's easy for us to sit back now and say what a good coach Terry is but it was clear he was even at that stage. He wasn't frightened to try out new ideas, different formations and tactics. He helped the younger boys through into the first team and of course got us to a Cup Final as a Second Division side, then promotion to Division One.

That was a fantastic achievement in a short space of time. He had great man management skills, he'd have a laugh and a joke at the right time but he knew when to pull away and become the manager."

What do you remember about your first goal?

"It was against Fulham, I must've driven it in from five yards out! It was at Craven Cottage and we won two-nil. I think I got a nose bleed from being that far up the pitch!"

Rangers were always the centre of controversy because of the plastic pitch in the eighties - people complained that the Astro-turf gave us an advantage. Did it?

"Yes, it was an advantage because we were used to the surface. But I think the surface made us better players because our passing had to be so accurate, you had to find your team mate otherwise the ball would fly off the pitch. It was challenging for us though as we had to switch between plastic and grass every week, but you could sense teams didn't fancy it when they came to Loftus Road.

The burns were the worst part, especially for players like me. If there was a tackle that needed to be made I'd go in for it but when I got up my legs would be in bits. You'd go to bed, then wake up on Sunday morning and the sheets would be stuck to your legs where the burns had been weeping during the night.

The funniest player was Michael Robinson, he didn't get a single plastic burn during his Rangers career until his last game, then he fell over and ripped himself to pieces. But he only suffered the pain once, I went through it every week!"

We took Tottenham as far as we could during the 1982 Cup Final, can you remember what the spirit was like before the games?

"The first game was amazing. I remember watching Cup Finals on TV as a kid then going down the park with my mates and pretending to be the man-of-the-match, so it was like a dream come true. All these thoughts go through your mind and you're tossing and turning all Friday night, I didn't sleep well at all. Then you have all the build up throughout the day, getting off the coach with the TV cameras pointing at you, just like you remember watching as a kid - so for it to happen to me so young seemed unreal.

On the day I wasn't nervous, I was just excited. The biggest thing for me was seeing the twin towers, it hit me just how many people were going to watch the game. The one thing I will never ever forget is the noise when we walked out of the tunnel, it was just amazing, a fantastic feeling. I could see my wife in the crowd, I still don't know how, but I picked her out of 100,000 people straight away.

We did okay in the first game and I couldn't move until Tuesday, as I was absolutely shattered. It was surreal, at the reception on the Saturday night we suddenly realised we had to play another Cup Final in a few days time.

Obviously we got beaten in the replay, and I vividly remember when Spurs got their goal with about fifteen minutes to go, I was playing and crying at the same time. The emotions you experience going through something like that are amazing. But we won so many fans with the way we tried to play in that game and I think that helped a lot of players' careers.

For a Second Division club it was an amazing achievement, every player's dream is to play in a Cup Final at Wembley, we did it and no one can ever take that away from us. It hurts to lose and it hit me hard, but a few weeks later we realised what an achievement it was."

We romped the Second Division the following season, what was that like to be a part of?

"It was great. The Cup Final gave us a lot of confidence and we went into the season with the right attitude - there was no way we were going to stay in that division. You could sense the confidence in the squad, we performed week in, week out and we were very worthy champions."

The year after that we finished fifth in Division One and qualified for the UEFA Cup. That might have taken others by surprise but did the squad know they were capable of European football?

"Our first game back in the big time was Manchester United away. I knew Ray Wilkins when I was growing up and he played for United in that game. We lost three-one but played well and afterwards Ray said to me that if we could continue to play like that we'd have a very good season - which

1985: Waddock on the ball against Everton at Goodison Park

we did. We knew what a good squad we had and we'd been together for a while. So everyone knew each other's strengths and weaknesses and we worked really hard together to achieve the success we had."

Did it hit the squad hard when Venables went off to Barcelona?

"It did, but if a club like Barcelona comes knocking at your door you take the job! I think everybody was pleased for him. It's the same with players really, if Manchester United or Liverpool had come in for someone, you'd be disappointed they were leaving, but understand why they were going. I just consider myself lucky to have worked for the fella, he improved me as a player."

He didn't want to take any of you off to Spain with him then?

"[Laughs] Maybe if he had gone to a smaller club! He had the pick of the world's best players, and as good as we were, I don't think we fell into that category at that time!"

Terry Venables was replaced by Alan Mullery, but he didn't last very long. It must have been hard for him to follow someone like Venables, but why didn't things click under his regime?

"Terry was always going to be a hard act to follow, whoever stepped in. Mullery was a good coach in his own right, he was good to me when he was here and he's said nice things about me since I've retired, but it was always going to be difficult for him to follow someone like Terry after the success he'd had."

One game I wanted to ask you about from the eighties that every one remembers was the 5-5 draw with Newcastle, then I looked it up and realised you didn't play in it!

"[Laughs] Yeah, I was injured at the time. I was sitting in the Upper Loft, I used to get my complimentary tickets and change them to go and sit with the fans and got to know quite a few people.

But the Newcastle match was a remarkable game, fantastic to watch. From being 4-1 down we came back and drew 5-5 which was amazing. What a comeback!"

Did you get any peace sitting with the supporters?

"The people I sat with just knew me as Gary the supporter whenever I was injured, I always had a great rapport with the crowd which was fantastic for me. They were great to me and I always used to enjoy hearing their views and they would ask me mine. To me that's what football is all about. Not every player would feel comfortable doing the same though."

2002: QPR's Centre of Excellence Director, Gary Waddock

Another high scoring affair was when Rangers got eliminated from Europe in 1984. You played in the game where we got knocked out, but after taking a 6-2 lead to Partizan Belgrade it must have been a huge shock to get dumped out of the UEFA Cup?

"I missed the first leg at Highbury [QPR were forced to play away from Loftus Road due to the plastic pitch] as I hadn't quite recovered from my broken ankle and I watched the game from the stands. We did remarkably well against a very well known team.

Alan Mullery brought me back for the return leg as he knew the game was going to be a bit of a battle and he wanted me out there. There was a very intimidating atmosphere over in Yugoslavia, as we walked out onto the pitch there were ball bearings being thrown at us - then we got battered on the night.

On that performance Belgrade thoroughly deserved to go through and it opened our eyes as to how the game could be played - it was a good learning curve for us. After the first game we thought we had a big enough lead to get us through, we prepared properly, but the result showed us what happens if you get off to a bad start in the return leg in Europe."

Shortly afterwards you suffered the knee injury that was thought to have finished your professional career. Everyone was telling you that you'd never play at a high level again, the medical people had written you off and the club's insurance company had issued the compensation payment which means a pro has to call it a day. That wasn't the end of the Gary Waddock story by a long stretch was it? Yours must be one of the most remarkable comeback stories in modern day football - what kept your dream alive?

"I wanted to prove everybody wrong. When I first damaged my medial ligaments and I learned the extent of the damage, my only concern was whether I'd play again - my medical advisor said 'yes I would'. But after about ten months the recovery hadn't gone as planned and the club made a decision that they thought I couldn't play any more. So I returned to the same advisor. I said to him, 'you told me that I'd play again...', he just looked at me and replied, 'yes, you will, but I didn't say at what level' - so he'd completely covered himself.

I wanted to prove a point, people obviously thought I couldn't be the same player again, but I thought I could be, I thought I could even improve as a player, but a decision was made to claim the insurance money and it left me without a career.

My only options, if I wanted to remain a player, were to play in the Second Division up in Scotland or go to America or Europe. Rodney Marsh at Tampa Bay Rowdies asked if I'd like to go over to the States and there were a number of German, Dutch and Belgian clubs who were interested, so in the end, I had to weigh up what I thought was the best route back for me personally. My goal was always to come back, my dream was to play at the highest possible level that I could and prove people wrong, because I am that kind of person. There was no way I was going to lay down and die, anyone who has seen me play will know that.

I felt that Europe was my best option, if you can make a name for yourself it's not too far away for people back home to hear about you. I then had three trials, two in Belgium with Standard Liege and Charleroi then another with Vitesse in Holland. They all went very well and I wanted to focus on just those three, then I wanted to make a decision, not them, me, I was intent on doing what was best for myself.

In the end I picked Charleroi, I felt it was right for me and they initially offered me a six month contract even though they warned me it may take that long for me to get into the first team. But by the end of the pre-season matches I was in the first team, after just three weeks. So I went in to see the Club President and asked him if he'd rip my contract up, he agreed. I then had another medical and they said my knee was fit enough to be offered a two year deal."

That must have been a great day for you, to hear that good news after all the previous knock-backs.

"I can't thank them enough to be honest with you, they were still taking a risk with me as I could have broken down after three months. Obviously the standard isn't as high as it is over here, but they'd given me the chance to build up my confidence again and get the strength back in my knee.

I stayed there for almost two years, then my mother-in-law died which was obviously a very difficult time, especially for my wife living over in Belgium. It was also around that time that I started to hear rumours that I was being watched by a couple of English teams.

By chance I bumped into Jack Charlton at an after-dinner presentation at Gerrards Cross, we got chatting and he asked me over to play in a game in Ireland. Tony Cascarino was there too and when he went back to Millwall he got the ball rolling for me. Millwall asked me to come over to London for a couple of days training to see if I could stand up to the training, but it was a development that put me in a very difficult situation with my club in Belgium. I went to the Charleroi President and explained the situation, in reality I would have been happy to stay at the club for the rest of my career, but it was my goal to get back to England.

The first day training with Millwall I put in a crunching tackle and I think that must have made their minds up because the next day the manager called me in and offered me a two-year contract. There were still a couple of stumbling blocks to get over though, firstly Millwall had to pay Charleroi a transfer fee and had to pay nearly all of the insurance fee back before I was allowed to play in the Football League again - but they did it.

So I'd completed my comeback, people said I couldn't but I was back even though getting into the Millwall side was going to be tough with Terry Hurlock and Les Briley ahead of me who are club legends.

Gerry Francis then asked me if I'd like to come and train back at QPR. The whole place had changed since I'd left the club, completely different medical staff, a different Chairman and a new Board. So when Gerry subsequently offered me a one year contract to come back to Loftus Road I accepted because I didn't feel Rangers was run by the people who had made decisions about ending my career a few seasons previously.

Gerry Francis was the one who asked me to start getting involved in developing the youth players and I am very grateful to him for that - but I wasn't happy just playing in the reserves and coaching the youngsters, I wanted to be back playing first team football.

Then Glen Hoddle came in for me when he was Swindon manager, remember, all this attention for someone with a supposed bad knee. Then, to top it all, I was called up to the full Republic of Ireland squad again! Christ almighty, I was the happiest man in the world. I was even initially called up for the Ireland World Cup squad for Italia '90."

Was that the proudest moment in your career?

"Well, I've been lucky enough to have a number to choose from - playing for QPR's first team at seventeen was a great achievement, then representing Ireland, then playing in the FA Cup Final in 1982, getting promoted to the top flight the next season and playing abroad - but getting married and having a little girl supersede all of those achievements."

Today you are totally involved in developing QPR's youth system and helping feed the first team with fresh talent. Looking at the kids at the club today, do you feel the club has a bright future?

"Very much so, yes. We've already seen a steady stream of youth players going on to make their first team debuts and there are still a lot of good players coming through.

Queen's Park Rangers has always produced good, young players and I think it is even more important today, in light of ITV Digital's collapse and the club's administration problem, that this football club cultivates it's own new players.

By doing that the young players have a feel for the club as well, their hearts are in it. We've got some fantastic people working in the Youth set-up and we all play a part, I believe the club's future is very bright."

Phil Parkes saves from Everton's Bob Latchford at Loftus Road

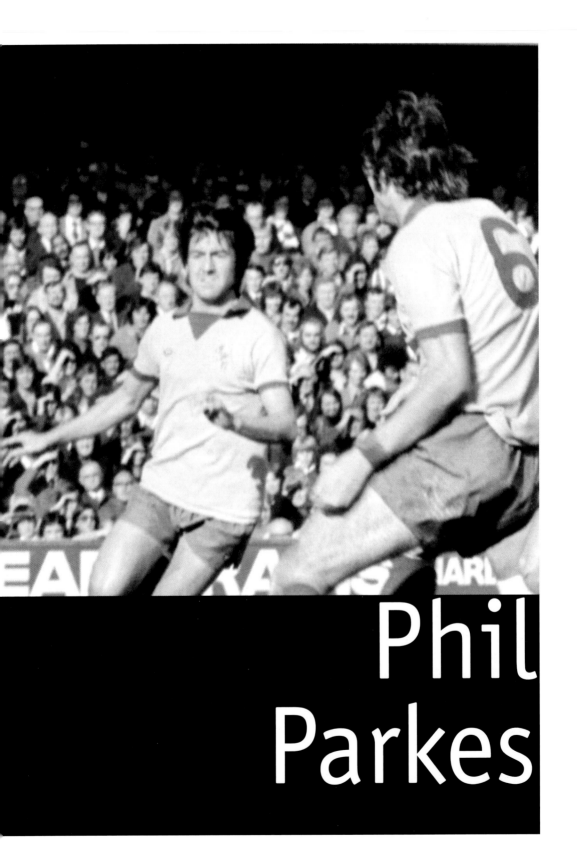

Phil
Parkes

Date: Thursday 31st October, 2002
Venue: TGI Friday, Reading
Era: 1970-1979 Appearances: 406 Goals: 0

If you follow the Alan Hansen school of football logic ("you have to build from the back") then you couldn't have built them bigger or better than Phil Parkes. When I met him my first thought was "Jesus Christ, look at the size of him!" At 6ft 3in Parkes is an imposing figure, and you can appreciate exactly why so little got past him between the sticks. He also has the biggest hands I've ever shaken!

Phil joined Rangers (the English ones, read on that will make sense) from Walsall in 1970 aged just twenty years old and immediately established himself as the number one 'keeper at Loftus Road - a status he would retain throughout his nine seasons at the club. Phil admits today that if he hadn't been dropped straight in the deep end he doubts whether he "would have become the same keeper".

Phil would of course watch many superb moments play out in front of him at Loftus Road, including the fantastic 1975-76 season and the UEFA Cup run that followed the next year. He proved to be a vital piece in the Rangers jigsaw that was put together by Dave Sexton and Gordon Jago.

Unfortunately Phil left the club in 1979, moving onto London rivals West Ham in a £565,000 deal that was a world record fee for a goalkeeper at the time. It appears that he didn't really want to go and was a little surprised by the move, however, having paid only £15,000 to sign him nine years earlier, the huge profit appeared to be something that Rangers' chairman, Jim Gregory, had to reluctantly accept.

Of course Phil's time at West Ham and the success he enjoyed there, arguably eclipses his achievements at Rangers - he won the FA Cup and Second Division Championship during a very eventual couple of seasons that also saw The Hammers reach a League Cup final.

Parkes eventually finished his career at Ipswich and moved into coaching with the Tractor Boys before returning to do a similar job at QPR under Gerry Francis in 1992. Phil has now left football completely and runs a successful building business.

Despite his success away from Loftus Road, Phil will never forget his time at QPR. He describes his seventies side as not only the best team he ever played in, but also the best he ever saw play. Some compliment.

Rangers have had some great goalkeepers over the years, Reg Allen and David Seaman are names that spring to mind, however, in most fans' minds, Phil Parkes would be the all time number one, number one.

Most kids grow up dreaming of being England's centre-forward, did you always want to be a 'keeper?

"Always, I went in goal at every opportunity from as far back as I can remember. I found I just had a natural talent for diving and not hurting myself, I even used to dive around in the street. I learnt how to fall from an early age. Plus I hated running, that helped me decide to go in goal!"

You joined Rangers from Walsall in 1970, what were you looking for from the move?

"Well I remember I was down in Weymouth on holiday with my wife, staying in a boarding house, when this telegram arrived for me. I saw it pushed under our bedroom door, so I opened it and it said 'ring Walsall immediately'. Obviously there were no mobile phones in those days so I walked down to the nearest phone box and the secretary said the club had received an offer from Queen's Park Rangers for me and I had to come back from my holiday straight away.

This is the gospel truth, I told him 'look, I'm on holiday, I'm back on Saturday, I'm not interrupting my holiday for anybody, besides I'm not interested in moving to Scotland anyway!' He paused and replied, 'Phil, Queen's Park Rangers is in London...' I wish the ground could have swallowed me up, I didn't even know where QPR was.

But the whole move happened really quickly after that, it was all done and dusted in a day and it turned out to be a brilliant move."

How did you find the club when you arrived?

"The funny thing was that I was just a quiet lad from the Midlands but the club put me up with Mike Ferguson for the first week of pre-season training, I was rooming with him in a hotel.

I didn't drink then, but this guy would take me out round all the pubs in Hammersmith and round The Bush and have about nine pints a night! I was out every night until about two o'clock in the morning, I couldn't believe it, this was pre-season and I was completely knackered.

That arrangement didn't last too long, I then found some fabulous digs in Wendall Road, Shepherd's Bush with a couple who became like a second mother and father to me."

You didn't exactly have a dream debut did you?

"I played well I thought. We lost 3-1 to Leicester, but I didn't have a problem with any of the goals - Peter Shilton was in goal at the other end. I remember being nervous, in fact I've always been nervous, but I think that's a good thing, it means you never get complacent. Coming to Rangers was a fairy story for me really, I could have moved to the club and been

Parkes makes a save against Arsenal at Highbury

stuck in the reserves for three years, but if that had happened I doubt whether I would have become the same 'keeper.

I seemed to earn the respect of most of the players quite quickly, we had a fairly young side and I became big buddies with a lot of the lads."

Your first Rangers manager, Les Allen, got the chop soon after you arrived and was replaced by Gordon Jago. How was that?

"I love Gordon, he was a great diplomat, but he was frightened about upsetting people and as a manager he was too nice really. His assistant, Bobby Campbell, was the nasty piece of work, he wound everyone up and was the bad cop. Then Gordon would come along and smooth everything over. Gordon was a good manager."

You played with some great, plus a few not so great, defenders at QPR, who did you feel most comfortable playing behind?

"You're right, there were a few, the first was Vic Mobley, then Ronnie Hunt and Frank Sibley, but I've got to say the best was Frank McLintock, he was amazing. His enthusiasm for the game, especially at his age, was brilliant.

I think he was such an inspiration to everyone at the club - he had such an appetite for the game. Frank was the oldest player in the side, but he would run around as if he was the youngest. David Webb was great too. I remember if I was going in high to catch a ball, Webby would always jump into the centre-forward, block him, then fall on the floor in a heap. The referee would look confused then just wave play on - he did it all the time. Webb was a great player to have in the side and a funny man."

You played over 400 games for Rangers, which one do you remember most vividly?

"I'll always remember the UEFA Cup match away in Cologne when we were 3-0 up from the first leg. In the return Don Masson scored again after about eight minutes, then things went a bit pear shaped.

They had this really tricky winger and Dave Clement, who was marking him, didn't really like taking prisoners. He was a hard, hard man so he clobbered him a few times, but in the end he got sent off. From being 4-0 up on aggregate it became like the Alamo and after half an hour they'd pulled it back to 4-4.

Somehow we managed to hang on and didn't let another one in though and when the referee blew the final whistle we knew we were through on the away goals rule. But all their players thought there was going to be extra time - they didn't know the rules. There was absolute uproar, they were all up in arms and complaining to the referee. The Radio commenta-

2002: The unmistakable Phil Parkes in Reading

tor, Ron Jones, gave me a tape of the game which I listen to now and again and it sounds like we never got in their half once, [laughs] they could have probably taken their 'keeper off and brought on another striker.

How on earth we ever got through that night I will never know. It was a similar night over in Athens when we got to the Quarter Finals but unfortunately that night we got knocked out on penalties after taking a decent lead away.

I've never been to a more intimidating place than Athens in all my life though, it was far worse that night than anything I experienced travelling with England. I remember seeing a lot of their supporters holding up knives and gesturing that they were going to cut our throats with them.

They were throwing stones and spitting at the coach as we arrived too, it was really horrible. David Webb missed the penalty that put us out that night, he put it about six feet over the crossbar."

You coached other goalies when you gave up playing, how did your own methods compare to those when you arrived at QPR?

"To be honest I think QPR was quite revolutionary with regard to training their goalies. Gordon Jago brought in Steve Burtenshaw to help out with new ideas in training and he was brilliant.

He was the one who started the really intensive training for 'keepers and when he left I started working on routines myself. I think QPR were ahead of any other club in the country. When Dave Sexton arrived, he loved what he saw on the training pitch."

From a 'keeper's view, what was it like to be part of Rangers' 75-76 Championship run-in?

"It was amazing to me because I could see everything happening in front of me. More often than not I'd start the moves off, I normally rolled the ball out instead of kicking it up field. Dave Sexton brought that in, he said 'why kick the ball and make the odds only 50-50 that one of our players will win it?' So the players would make space for themselves and I'd roll it to them and build from the back.

It seems obvious now, but then we were seen as different. It made for more entertaining football which the crowds appreciated I think. Missing out that season is my biggest disappointment in football though, we were by far the best team that season and Liverpool stole the title."

Were there any forwards who really worried you back then?

"No, not really. There were a few players you'd come up against, people like Joe Jordan at Manchester United, who you knew would hit you - but you'd just hit him back so it didn't matter. You would smash into him and he would smash into you, but nobody would go bleating to the referee.

Most players were hard but fair, but there were a few, Hugh Curran at Oxford for example, who would always whack you in the back. I thought he was a coward because he wouldn't come face-on to you, he thought he would get hurt. [Laughs] I never did get the chance to get my own back with him!"

You made your England debut in Sir Alf Ramsey's last game in charge of the side didn't you?

"Yeah, it was against Portugal, I'll always remember winning that first cap. Probably the most memorable England game I was involved with was that infamous game at Wembley against Poland.

I was in the squad for that game and we were all so gutted to miss out on a trip to the World Cup. I remember going to a club in Staines called Sergeant Pepper's with Tony Currie and a few of the other players after the game to drown our sorrows."

Rangers sold you to West Ham in February 1979 for £550,000, which was a world record fee for a goalie at the time. Did that put you under a lot of pressure?

"None what so ever. The way I looked at it was that the West Ham manager, John Lyall, had signed me and if the move didn't work out it was him under all the pressure."

Did you have agents negotiating the deal for you back then?

"No I did it myself, but it wasn't that daunting because I didn't want to move and it was up to John Lyall to sell the idea of moving to West Ham to me. Jim Gregory told me that he didn't want me to go before the end of the season, or at least not until he knew QPR were safe from relegation, but as West Ham were interested he said I should speak to them out of courtesy.

I'd never been in that situation before, but I saw John Lyall and he was brilliant - the offer doubled my wages and the bonuses were amazing. But then I turned to him and said 'that's great John, but we've got a problem, I don't really want to leave. I'm happy where I am'.

I'd just moved house, my kids were settled at school, all my friends lived near me and there was no M25 so the thought of driving all the way across London didn't appeal to me. John thought about it for a bit, then said to me, 'okay, we'll move the training start time back until 10 o'clock'. But that was still no good to me because I'd have to leave my house at 6 o'clock in the morning as I would have to get to East London by train.

Then he offered to move training back even further and start at 10.30. I thought if the guy was prepared to bend over backwards for me and even risk upsetting all his other players' routines, he must want me to go pretty desperately, so I decided I'd go for it. Things at QPR weren't that good at the time and we were struggling under Steve Burtenshaw after he became manager, none of the players had a lot of respect for him, so I thought the time was right to move on.

But from QPR's point of view they only paid £15,000 for me, they'd had nine good years and were being offered a huge amount of money. Jim Gregory still wasn't convinced though, but I think his son, who was on the QPR board at the time, talked him round into thinking what a good business deal it was.

Jim was brilliant about it, he thanked me for being such a good servant for the club and then gave me a Golden Handshake because he said I missed out on a testimonial."

How do you compare your career at West Ham to your time at QPR?
"Quite differently, because I eclipsed everything that I'd achieved at Rangers within three years at West Ham. We won the FA Cup Final, played in the Charity Shield, got through to the League Cup Final and won the Second Division Championship.

But although I was part of a fantastic team at West Ham and achieved a lot, it still doesn't compare to the Rangers side of 1976. To me that 1975-76 QPR side is the best team I've ever played in, or ever seen play."

I hear you're becoming a Loftus Road regular again?
"[Laughs] Sort of, I've been invited to get involved with the match-day hospitality at Loftus Road. Meeting and greeting corporate guests, speaking about the old times and chatting to fans about the good times.

I really enjoy it."

1992: Alan McDonald goes head-to-head with Mark Hughes

Alan
McDonald

Date: Saturday 22nd June, 2002
Venue: Alan's house, Swindon, Wiltshire
Era: 1981-1997 Appearances: 476 Goals: 18

Ask any Queen's Park Rangers supporter to list their greatest ever side and chances are Alan McDonald will be in it. He was Rangers through and through and the fact that supporters from two generations would tell you the same makes it even more incredible.

Alan admits that he "wasn't one of the most gifted players in the world" but the passion with which he played and the desire he showed on the pitch was exactly how every fan imagines themselves playing if they were ever lucky enough to live out the dream. He played with a fan's spirit and we loved him for it.

QPR came dangerously close to never signing Alan, as he talks about in the interview, apart from Manchester United offering him terms, McDonald had already agreed to sign for Wolves when he came for trials at Rangers. Fortunately blue and white was his destiny and the rest is history.

Alan saw it all in during his career at QPR, promotions, relegations, cup finals and no less than eight managers. McDonald was always a loyal club servant and he clearly still loves Queen's Park Rangers today but it was so regrettable that his exit from Loftus Road wasn't as glorious as his sixteen years had been.

Alan answered everything asked of him extremely candidly, some of which he hadn't discussed in public before. QPR fans hold Macca in the highest esteem, and whilst he had his fair share of good times and bad times at QPR, it is clear that the respect is mutual.

It is also apparent that being so fondly thought of touches him - in his words, "it makes up for not having cups and medals". How many modern-day footballers would say something like that?

All footballers start off playing for the love of the game, the simple fun of kicking a ball around, but in today's money driven football world it seems all too easy for them to forget why they fell in love with the game in the first place.

Macca always played with that playground passion, that sense of pride and determination and it's great to see it is still with him today. Mention Queen's Park Rangers and his eyes light up, mention Stewart Houston and, well...

Alan is currently working as a part-time coach with the Northern Ireland under-21 team which is the perfect reward for his endeavours on the pitch for his country - McDonald won fifty-two caps while he was at Rangers.

So what have you been doing since you retired from playing football?

"Well obviously I was at Swindon Town, where I finished my career and moved onto the coaching staff. I was coaching the reserves and when the club went into administration the assistant manager was made redundant. I ended up being acting assistant manager, reserve team manager, helping prepare the kit, doing the boots, the lot!

The club was in such bad financial trouble, they were losing something like £26,000 a week so they made fifteen of the staff redundant and we all had to muck in. My idea was to leave Jimmy Quinn, the manager, as much time as possible to concentrate on running the first team, which was virtually impossible because the financial restrictions were astronomical.

Then Jim got the sack and a couple of days later I left on principle. It was actually at the QPR game. I took charge of the team for the day because Jim was scouting, it was there I found out that Colin Todd was at the match, so I made a few enquires and found out that Swindon had arranged for Colin Todd to join with his whole backroom staff. That brought everything to a head and I left a couple of days later.

From there I took a year out because, to be honest with you, I got totally disillusioned with coaching because of the way things had turned out at Swindon - the way things had been done. We felt we'd done the best we could for the club, tried our best to slash the budget and tried to do everything for the benefit of the club. Basically we felt we'd been stabbed in the back, so it made me very cynical at the time.

Since then things have sort of looked up, for the last eighteen months I've been working with Roy Miller who is the manager of the Northern Ireland under twenty-one team and I've been coaching with them. We've had nine or ten qualifying games in the last eighteen months, which was a brilliant experience for me.

Also, Sammy McIlroy's [Northern Ireland's International manager] assistant Jim Harvey has other commitments as he's the manager at Morecambe, so when he's away I've also been coach for the full Northern Ireland team which has been brilliant.

Obviously I know most of the players but it was great working with the full team because I played for them for ten and a half years - it's nice being back involved.

I've also been doing work for the Press Association as a football analyst at live games. I report all the match facts back to a controller on the mobile, then Sky Sports use all the information. All the tackles, free kicks, corners and throw-ins.

I've been doing that about a year which has been great because it's part-time and keeps me involved in football. In that respect I'm still really involved in the game and to be honest I'm involved in a capacity which suits me - the part-time jobs dove tail together perfectly."

Are you still in touch with anyone from your time at QPR?
"When I was coaching I went back to QPR for a few games, when Gerry Francis was the manager. In fact at one stage I spoke to Gerry about going back to Loftus Road, but with the desperate financial restrictions at QPR, it didn't happen. It was sad to see - it's heartbreaking.

I've had a couple of offers to go back and work part time in the academy and the school of excellence but to be honest with you I'm living in Swindon and I didn't think it was fair on my five year old little boy Joshua or my wife if I was travelling up and down every day. I've lived in Swindon for three years now and my son Joshua is settled so we're going to stay here.

I spoke to Nick Blackburn when the manager's job came up last time but they decided to give it to Ian Holloway which made sense - although Ian's had a difficult job because the finances were in mess. Hopefully they can get that really sorted out because it's too good a club to see struggle."

It's been a struggle, but Ian Holloway's done remarkably well.
"He has, and I sympathise with Ian wholeheartedly because I know exactly what it's like. The two years I was on the coaching staff at Swindon there wasn't a day when we weren't concerned about money.

Unfortunately, instead of being able to deal with team matters, there was always some financial situation which arose that affected the manager or the coaching staff. So instead of devoting your whole time to football matters you have to deal with financial problems, like players knocking on the door saying 'are we getting paid this month?'

The last thing you want to be doing as a coach or manager is talking about day-to-day finances because you're trying to concentrate on other things. So I sympathise 110% with Ian Holloway, I think he's done a great job in very, very difficult circumstances. For me, as an outsider looking in, when you look back to the good old days when we were playing in the Premier League, it's soul destroying to look at the club now. It's a skeleton of the club I knew.

Some of the staff are still there, I know them very well and I speak to them from time to time. But it's heartbreaking when you think back to the things we achieved and the good times we had - it's very difficult to take for the supporters."

Better times are ahead now we're out of administration.
"Well I hope so, it's a fabulous club and I spent seventeen and a half years there. I had a few bad moments with a couple of managers, but

overall I don't think there's very much I would change if I had my time over again.

I was always very happy at QPR and I was treated very well by the fans and the staff. It still has a very special place in my heart and it always will do. The first result I look for every Saturday is QPR's."

Going back to your early days, how exactly did you end up at QPR in the first place?

"Well I played for the Northern Ireland schoolboy international team who were European Champions back in 1978 and had more or less agreed to sign for Wolves. But a dear friend of mine, Bill Smith, who was the QPR scout in Northern Ireland, persuaded me otherwise. Bill was very big friends with Frank Sibley and persuaded Ian Stewart to come to QPR too.

Bill said to me 'do you want to go to QPR?' I said I wasn't really fussed so he said 'look at it this way, it's a free holiday, QPR want to see you, go over for a week, do a bit of training and see London'. I said 'okay, I'll go over for a free week in London!' I was so impressed, everyone was so nice and the club was so good to me. I changed my mind and agreed to sign for QPR.

When I signed in 1979 Tommy Docherty was the manager and Rangers were second from bottom in the league. The thing that appealed to me was QPR was a fairly small club, it was friendly and the people were nice. I thought I had a good chance of making the grade.

I'd been to Manchester United twice on trial and they wanted to sign me, but I thought it was too big a club. When I went there for the weekend there was something like three hundred kids there.

I moved over in October 1979 and finished my last eight months of school in London. It was a nightmare because of the home sickness and I missed my friends and my family. I was meant to go to school three days a week, but most of the time I never bothered, I just wanted to train.

I'd just turned sixteen and was living in digs - it was an awful time. In hindsight I should have stayed at home, finished school then come over. But I guess it built my character, because I had to get on with it.

It was no good moaning. I was extremely homesick but it made me grow up very quickly, I was on my own and I had to stand on my own two feet.

Not long after that Ian Stewart joined the club so the two of us sort of stuck together. Basically, for the first two years, I struggled to settle down, but once I did, it was fine."

It's ironic that having almost signed for Wolverhampton Wanderers, you made your Rangers debut against them?

"That's right yeah, it was strange the way that happened. Bob Hazell got injured and I'd been hoping to get in the team - then all of a sudden my opportunity came out of the blue. It was a fabulous day, I remember Andy Gray was playing for Wolves and he cracked my rib during the match. But we beat them four-nil, Clive Allen scored a couple of cracking goals and John Burridge, who was at QPR when I signed, was in goal for Wolves. That was a tremendous day, because Wolves were a good team so it was great winning at Molineux."

Who did you support as a boy?

"I was never really a staunch one team supporter, I flipped from team to team really. I used to support Leeds, when they had that fabulous team in the seventies, and funnily enough I supported QPR for a while when they had the brilliant team with Don Givens and Gerry Francis. So I went through a period of supporting QPR.

Then I went through a stage of supporting Manchester United and I still have a little hankering for them. In Northern Ireland kids tend to support one of two teams, Liverpool or Manchester United, but I supported whoever was doing well."

Did you have any idols, anyone who inspired you to be a footballer?

"Yes, local people, like George Best. Pat Jennings was also a massive hero of mine, I was very fortunate to play several internationals with him. Jimmy Nicholl, the former Manchester United full back, too.

Particularly George Best though, he's an absolute legend back home, he was an inspiration. George played in my testimonial at QPR and I played in his at Windsor Park which was an unbelievable honour for me.

Jimmy and his family used to live about three hundred yards from my Mum and Dad. Jimmy went to the same school as me - although he was about eight years older he played football with my brothers."

A bit later in your career now - the 1986 League Cup Final. [Alan laughs] What do you remember from that? Why did it go so wrong?

"We had a phenomenal run through, we beat Nottingham Forest, Chelsea and Liverpool in the Semi Final. To be fair Oxford beat some great teams as well, but I think we just froze on the day to be honest. It's probably the one disappointment I look back on most.

I can remember it like it was yesterday. The support was phenomenal, it was a beautiful day and the build up had been tremendous.

It was a crazy year for me, in my first full season as a regular I played in a Cup Final for QPR and Northern Ireland qualified for the World Cup in Mexico. In the space of six months I'd gone from being a reserve team player to appearing in the World Cup and a major final at Wembley.

To be totally honest Oxford were by far the better team, they did deserve to win but we never got going whatsoever - I was just shocked that we never got out of the traps. We played so well through the whole competition but when it came to the final we might as well have stayed in the dressing room. The one game that matters and we play like we've never bloody played together before."

Okay something more cheery then - what would you say was your proudest moment at QPR?
"I think just before kick-off prior to the Oxford final to be honest. I can remember being on the pitch at the start of the game and looking around, there must have been forty thousand QPR supporters there. When I saw the blue and white end I can remember thinking how tremendous it looked.

That particular season would be the highlight of my career as a footballer, I made my international debut in October 1985, winning away in Romania then we drew with England and qualified for the 1986 World Cup. So those particular six months were the proudest moments of my career - but one of the worst at the same time with that Wembley fiasco.

There were so many good points during that era, I can remember beating Manchester United four-one on New Year's Day and Dennis Bailey got a hat-trick. Dennis was a national hero!

I'm also proud of our achievements while Gerry was the manager. We finished fifth then ninth and we had a very good team. A very, very good team. For QPR, one of the smaller Premier League teams at the time, to finish that high was a fantastic achievement, for us it was like winning the League Championship.

That was probably the golden period when Gerry was there. We had a fabulous team, a great spirit and real good camaraderie around the club."

You stayed with QPR for thirteen years, did you have offers to leave Loftus Road?
"At one stage there were several teams interested and there were very strong links with Tottenham, Manchester United and Chelsea. To be honest with you I was always happy at QPR though. We got well paid and we had a good team - it was a good club.

I had a few disagreements with a couple of managers, but you're going to get those no matter where you are. There were also times where I wasn't playing too well, but at the end of the day, I was always very happy at Queen's Park Rangers.

Over the thirteen years, there was probably a period of one year in separate parts where I felt a bit disillusioned or unhappy. A month here, a month there. There was one stage where I thought seriously about leaving,

I'd had a run in with a certain manager and I just thought maybe it's time to go. But that sorted itself out.

On the whole I'd say the reason I didn't leave is because I was happy. The backroom people were fabulous too - QPR through and through and really nice people.

The club helped me through a difficult period in my life and I think you've always got to give something back. So I thought 'I'm happy here, I'm playing well, I'm in the top division, it's a good club and we've got a good team.'

Okay, we sold players like David Seaman and Paul Parker but you had to be realistic. QPR had to sell players to survive and the players we were buying as replacements were good players too."

We used to sell someone for two million quid then use the money to buy three or four new players didn't we?
"That's right, everyone went crazy when we sold Les Ferdinand, but that was brilliant business. QPR got Les for about twenty-five grand and sold him for six million quid.

We got Paul Parker for about £250,000 and sold him for a fortune - the same with Dave Seaman. But we always signed good replacements.

I was extremely happy though - I knew the grass wasn't always greener on the other side. I could have moved and got more money but I was already on decent money and we were doing well.

I could have gone somewhere else, uprooted myself and ended up going through a bad period and realising it was a big mistake."

When you got towards the end, when you left the club, was that your choice?
"No."

That's the impression we got, most fans were pretty disgusted at how you were treated.
"My wife Tanya was absolutely distraught, totally gutted. It hit her more than it hit me. Sometimes you can't see clearly at the time and you don't discover things until later.

I was very disappointed in the way it was done, because I'd been speaking to Stewart Houston, who was the manager then, and he signed Steve Morrow from Arsenal to replace me just before the transfer deadline. I'd been playing really well all season and I think it was only John Spencer's signing that stopped me winning Player of the Year.

It was obvious then, Stewart dropped me and I couldn't understand why. I spoke to him about it and told him if he felt I wasn't good enough for him it was probably better that I moved on - which I didn't want to do. I was thirty-three then and I'd always wanted to finish my career at QPR, I felt I had a good couple of years left.

It went past the transfer deadline and I'd been speaking to Houston for about a month, but he wouldn't give me a straight answer. I kept saying 'what's happening, do you want me to leave? You haven't spoken to me about a new contract or my contract ending.' He said 'well if we can get into the play-offs, I'll think about giving you a new contract.'

I told him that was no good to me and I needed to know about my future. I remember saying, 'I'm an experienced player, I've got a wife, she's pregnant, I need to sort out what I'm going to be doing in the future.'

It just dragged on and on so I said, 'look Stewart, what's going on, do you want me to leave? Be honest with me because if I'm going to leave I can probably get myself a good club'. He said that he couldn't let me go so I stayed until the end of the season.

Then after the last game he spoke to all the players together and we had a meeting about the plans for the following season. I wasn't invited. He then called me into his office afterwards and said he wasn't offering me a new contract and that I was being released.

Looking back I was extremely disappointed with the way it was handled, I felt I deserved more. There were people at the club who had been there a few years and I felt they could've stuck up for me a bit more. I felt that at least they could have been a bit more upfront with me, but I don't hold grudges at the end of the day.

I knew I was getting old but I felt I had another two years left in me and I felt I could still play at that level. I went and played at Swindon the next year and we did really well.

It was just the way it was done, I felt I'd shown the club extreme loyalty. To be honest I would have been interested in doing part time coaching or anything to have stayed at QPR - it's a shame."

Well if it's any consolation you'll be remembered long after Stewart Houston is forgotten.

"It was about then that the club started going downhill, although not just because they got rid of me I hasten to add! That was the time when the rot started to set in.

Personally speaking, if I'm going to be totally honest with you, the rot set in when they got rid of Ray Wilkins. He came in during a difficult period, Gerry had left, everybody was concerned about that because Gerry had been so popular - so they appointed Ray to appease the fans.

Ray was a new manager and of course he made mistakes, we all make mistakes. Ray is one of the nicest guys you'll meet in football, a lovely man, but he joined as an inexperienced manager, in the middle of a difficult period. We got relegated from the Premier League, then three games into the new season, after winning two matches and drawing one, they sacked him even though we were top of the league!

I must admit the disappointment of being relegated was one of the lowest points of my life and we all went away in the summer to have a good, hard think. When we came back pre-season the whole squad had a long chat at the training ground with Frank Sibley and Ray Wilkins. I'd never seen a more determined bunch of lads, we felt we'd let Ray down - we'd let the club down.

Everybody worked hard to put things right - it's the hardest I'd ever seen us work in training. We were absolutely flying in pre-season and we started the season brilliantly. We went down and beat Portsmouth, we'd beaten Oxford at home and went up and drew with Wolves.

So we had seven points out of nine from three games, then they dropped the bombshell that they'd sacked Ray. The lads were so deflated after that, we couldn't understand why they'd done it."

People say that Stewart Houston's approach was slightly more, shall we say, authoritarian?

"Without a doubt. That's when the club was ruined in my opinion. There was £8m spent on players which was poorly spent. The atmosphere at the club was awful. Bitching started between the players, which I'd never seen before, we had a fabulous team spirit until then.

The atmosphere within the club was dreadful. Then, within a short period of time, I left along with Simon Barker and Ian Holloway. Genuine leaders on the pitch all leaving the club.

The events speak for themselves about what happened at the club. I have my views on it and they're very strong, but at the end the day I'm not going to throw any mud at people, but that's when the rot started to set in at the club and QPR are still paying the price for that year now."

The fans thought it felt like a huge weight had been lifted when Houston and Rioch were sacked, but do you feel the next appointment was a mistake too?

"Well, there's been a few. At the end of the day if Chris Wright was honest he'd hold his hands up and say things should have been done better. The thing you've got to remember with Chris is he was a supporter and it was the first experience he'd had of running a football club.

Chris Wright was a very inexperienced Chairman with an inexperienced manager in Ray Wilkins. When Ray got the sack, that accelerated the downward spiral and if you look at the events and the time scale, even a blind

1992: Macca goes in hard against Coventry City's Robert Rosario

1991: McDonald marshals his defence during the 2-2 draw at Crystal Palace

man can see that was where it started to go wrong. Anyway, that's past history. Hopefully the club can turn themselves round and get back to where they belong."

During your career who would you say was the best defensive partner you had at QPR?
"Terry Fenwick was a good player, but the best player I played with generally was Clive Wilson. I think Clive was an unbelievable full back.

People thought the loss of Les Ferdinand hurt the team, but I personally think that about when Clive went. You know there was no talk of Clive going, as far as we were concerned it was a real bolt out of the blue when he went to Tottenham.

Clive was such a gifted player, so skillful and a fabulous guy as well. I played with some cracking players though, like Mark Dennis. He was a brilliant defender even though he was a bit of a nutcase.

We had some great defenders over the years, Dave Seaman was a fabulous goalkeeper, Paul Parker, Danny Maddix was a good man-to-man marker, Dave Bardsley, Darren Peacock did well and went onto Newcastle and Steve Wicks - he was a good player too.

Glen Roeder was my hero when I first got into the team, but I'm spoilt for choice when I think about it."

You've had some great battles over the years, who would you say you enjoyed marking the most?
"Probably some of the biggest battles I ever had were with Mark Hughes, that was infamous. Mark was a tremendous professional, away from football he's a quiet guy a bit like myself, but it's different when you're on the pitch. Mark was always a battling player, very gifted, very strong and a fantastic goalscorer.

Obviously at times it went beyond the legal bounds from both of us but that's the way the games were played and you did whatever you could to try to win the game. It was always enjoyable because we always had a bit of a ding-dong!

When we used to play derbys with Chelsea I used to have a good battle with Kerry Dixon too, I always looked forward to them and I played against Kerry for Northern Ireland when he was in the England team."

You versus Mark Hughes was always brilliant to watch!
"When you get two players who are so committed to winning it gets a bit dirty and you have to give it out. The good thing with Mark was he'd give it out and he'd take it and get on with the game. I tend to think there was a lot of mutual respect for each other."

We haven't mentioned Jim Smith yet?

"Jim Smith was a good character, I got on brilliantly with him. Jim is of the old school. At times we'd have a right laugh, he's a lovely bubbly guy. He wasn't the best coach in the world but he had a good coach with him, he was a fantastic man manager though.

Jim really spoke his mind too, if he thought you were absolute crap he would say you were absolute crap! He wouldn't go round the houses, he would just come out and say it and I think people respected him for it. There were times when the cups when flying and he looked as if he was going to have a heart attack, his head would go bright red if he was fuming! He was a character Jim and there aren't enough of them left. "

What was Ian Holloway like as a player? Did he give the impression he'd succeed in management?

"He was a fabulous professional, he would probably say himself that he wasn't one of the most gifted players in the world but what you got from him was 100%, he would work his backside off.

I can remember coming back one pre-season and Ian had spent the summer training at an athletic club because he thought he wasn't fit enough, but he was the fittest guy at the club! We used to do runs in Richmond Park, about eight miles and he'd win hands down. Tremendous professional, unbelievable attitude and a lovely lad as well.

You always had the feeling he'd go into management, then he got an offer to play and coach at Bristol Rovers and it turned out to be the right move for him. Now he's doing a good job at QPR."

So what are you looking to do now? Are you happy with the two part-time roles or do you want to get back into football full time?

"I'm happy enough but I've applied for a couple of jobs including the Aldershot manager's job when it came up. I got an interview but Terry Brown, who was the Hayes manager, got it.

To be honest I'm not desperate to get into full-time football at the moment, if something came up that appealed to me I would look at it and apply, but I'm reasonably happy doing what I'm doing. I've got the European Championship qualifiers with Northern Ireland, that'll mean nine internationals in eleven months and will be pretty time consuming.

But I don't really want to uproot my family now, I'm getting too old for that. I guess it's a bit selfish but I don't want to be travelling two hours here, two hours there.

For nineteen years football has come first in my life and to be honest I want to start enjoying weekends at home for a change, playing and spending more time with my son."

What do think of the view of many Rangers fans that you are the greatest ever centre back to play at Loftus Road?

"[Laughs] They're easily pleased aren't they! A couple of friends of mine are still season ticket holders at Rangers and one of them sent me the programme when they printed 'the greatest team of all time' - I was in it.

That's a great honour for me. When I look back at my career I never really won anything with QPR, but when ordinary people on the street say you're the greatest ever centre back or you're in the best team ever, that makes up for not having cups and medals in my eyes.

I probably was never one of the most gifted players in the world but I gave what I had and it's nice to be appreciated.

I had some kids come up to me recently who said 'you're Alan McDonald, my Dad used to watch you and he says you were the best player at QPR'. They were about twelve years old and they knew me!

So it's nice if you affect people's lives and it's a great honour when they do these polls. It's very humbling."

1976: Gerry Francis during QPR's 2-1 win against Arsenal at Loftus Road

Gerry Francis

Date: Thursday 7th November, 2002
Venue: Penny Hill Park, Bagshot, Surrey
Era: 1969-1982 Appearances: 347 Goals: 65

It's very easy to remember Gerry Francis for the wrong reasons, younger fans may only think of his latterday management tenure, but the fact is he was one of the very finest footballers to ever pull on a blue and white shirt. Gerry spent the vast majority of his football life at Loftus Road, a period totalling over twenty years as player and manager.

The son of Brentford player, Roy Francis, he made his playing debut for QPR in 1969, aged just seventeen, coming off the bench against Liverpool in a two-one home defeat. Ironically, Liverpool would prove to be involved in other landmark events in Francis' Rangers' career.

Gerry only made the one appearance in his debut season and QPR would be relegated from Division One that year. Life in Division Two gave Gerry a chance to establish himself in Rangers' early seventies sides and he became a linchpin of the team that was to finally earn promotion back to the top flight in 1973. Gerry formed an instant footballing connection with Stan Bowles and the two terrorised defences across the land.

He would go on to become an integral part of Rangers' Championship chasing 1975-76 team that pushed Liverpool to the last day of the season and beyond. He would also score the goal of the season during the first match of that campaign, against the same Liverpool side who would ultimately leave Rangers empty handed.

It was shortly after that glorious season that Gerry suffered a back injury that would limit his first team appearances for the next few years. Once he'd recovered, Francis decided to move on to Crystal Palace for a season, before returning to Loftus Road again between 1980 and 1982.

Francis re-joined the club for a third time in 1991 and again in 1998 where he enjoyed some great successes as manager. In 1993 he guided the club to a record equalling fifth place in the top flight and in 1999 steered the club away from the bottom of Division One to safety after Rangers had looked doomed all season.

Interviewing Gerry was a pleasant experience and his time away from the game looks to have done him good - when he last left QPR Francis looked haggard and exhausted, when we met he was bright, cheery and full of stories.

Whether as a manager or a player, Gerry Francis has been involved in some key moments over the years. His loyalty to the club is unquestionable and he is rightly assured of a prominent place in the annals of Queen's Park Rangers' history.

You were only seventeen when you made your Rangers debut, how did you cope with the pressure at such a young age?

"It must have been very frightening at the time, but so much has happened since it's difficult to remember what was going through my mind back then. I know there was talk of me making my debut while I was still sixteen actually, there had been a few stories in the London evening 'papers, so there was a little bit of a build up to the day when I eventually played for the first team. Les Allen, who was the Rangers manager at the time, picked me to play my first game against a Liverpool side that included the likes of Ian St. John, Gordon Milne, Tommy Lawrence, Roger Hunt and Peter Thompson - they were a really good side. I came on as sub in the second half and the first thing I noticed was how quick the game was, I thought 'Christ Almighty!' I'll always remember the ball came to me in the middle of the pitch just after coming on, I wasn't really sure who was coming in behind me to be honest, but I let the ball run between my legs and turned. Fortunately there was nobody there at all and it worked out perfectly, the crowd all started cheering and clapping.

Although we lost the game 2-1 it was a nice debut. I had a couple more appearances including the away game at Chelsea in the final game of the season, but we were relegated by then. I made my first appearance in Division Two the next season down at Portsmouth and scored in a 3-1 win.

I always thought I was very, very lucky to become a player at Queen's Park Rangers, because in those days the club only took on a few apprentices because there was no government funded YTS system, the club had to totally fund their own youth system. My problem was that the secondary school I went to played rugby not football and although I was in the rugby side and even got involved with the England Youth team, the only chance I got to play football was on Sundays.

I actually wanted to go to Brentford because my dad played for them and I used to go and watch The Bees one week and QPR the next. I wrote to Brentford and asked for a trial but I never heard anything. Because Brentford ignored me it stopped me writing to Rangers as I thought I'd be treated the same way. Later in life, when I became a manager myself, I always made a point of replying to every letter I received.

In the end, my dad had a word with Rangers' Chief Scout, Derek Healey, and I was asked to come down for a few evening trials. I only just scraped through and the club wasn't really sure about me at all.

Three days after I signed as an apprentice I played for the reserves at Colchester and one of their players went straight through me, badly damaging my knee cartilage. I know QPR were really sick about that because at the time cartilage injuries weren't straight forward and I think the club were disappointed they'd signed me. I remember Derek Healey said some not very nice things about wishing he hadn't signed me. As a kid, they hurt, but I must say it made me determined to prove them wrong. That injury has caused me all kinds of problems with arthritis since and I've now got a metal plate in the back of my knee."

You must have been relieved to prove your doubters wrong?
"Fortunately I was back within about three months and the club's view-point changed from wishing they'd never signed me to giving me a pay rise. Apprentices weren't allowed to be paid appearance money at the time and I was only on £8 a week, then, in the second year they gave me an extra quid. After I'd played for the first team at least a dozen times, I was offered my first professional contract which was £15 per week, [laughs] then I went to £22 10s after that."

After your introduction to the first team you were in and out of the side and it wasn't until the start of the 1971-72 season that you became a regular. Was it frustrating as a youngster to be kept on the sidelines after being given a taste?
"Yeah it was and I was being played all over the place too. At one stage I was out on the right wing, while in the reserves, I was being played as a lone centre-forward - I always wanted to be a midfield player. But I was able to utilise those experiences as a manager and they helped me learn the game inside out - it was very informative.

So yes it was a bit frustrating having to wait after I'd had a taste of the first team, but I also knew there were a lot of good, experienced players around me in the squad when I was coming through."

You saw the transformation of the club both on and off the pitch in a short space of time, what was that like to witness?
"Well, Rangers had just won the League Cup before I arrived in 1967 and were definitely on the up, moving through the leagues, before coming back down with a bump in 1970 and having to start over again. But I saw the ground progress from having no real stands at all and having only one shower into what it is today. Jim Gregory made it all happen almost single handedly."

How would you compare football playing to football management?
"Football playing is easy, football management is a tough job which takes over your life completely. It's also hard to deal with squad members who aren't in the first team, you may have thirty or forty players at the club, but you can only pick eleven to play which leaves twenty or thirty of them hating you. When you walk into a room it all goes quiet because you

are The Boss and unfortunately you can't be one of the lads any more. You also play God in some ways, you can be very good friends with a certain player, then find you have to drop them or leave them out which ultimately affects their whole family. More often than not they want to leave for another club, uproot their kids from school, then move houses and all the grief that involves. So you've got to learn to cope with the pressures of the job, like dealing with the press. Phone calls in the middle of the night saying what the players are up to - I can't honestly say that management is enjoyable at all. Jumping up and down banging your head on the side of a dug-out isn't enjoyable to me, but what makes it all worthwhile is bringing the younger players through. Giving a leg-up to players like Les Ferdinand, Nigel Martyn, Trevor Sinclair and Sol Campbell - that was enjoyable."

Is winning just as enjoyable though?

"I think as a manager you get a greater feeling of enjoyment, because as a manager, in many ways, you are responsible for the whole victory not just an individual part of it. You've bought the players, picked the team, decided on formations and tactics - that is more of an accomplishment. The biggest problem is that there are only so many teams that can actually win anything. Queen's Park Rangers came fifth in the table and were the top London club, which is an unbelievable feat, but the next season you're expected to better it. I think we should have got an honour for achieving what we did at a smaller club who always have to sell its best players. You also know there's more bad times than good times in football management, once you get to a certain level, unless you're at Manchester United or Arsenal, everyone else are also-rans. But I was always happy at QPR and I would never have left if it weren't for the Thompson's. But they wanted me out - it was as simple as that."

Why do you think they had it in for you?

"Well I was causing a lot of trouble because they kept selling players and because of that they wanted me out quickly. They knew my temper, they knew I'd react to what they did.

They wound me up very well, especially inviting Rodney Marsh back to the club without telling me. It was in the press but the Chairman was unavailable to talk to me about it, then I turned up at the Liverpool game and there was Marshy sitting up in the stands which I reacted to. If bringing him to the club was such a good idea, why didn't the Thompson's see it through after I'd left? It was obviously staged.

Three weeks before that I got a phone call from the Wolves Chairman telling me that he'd been given permission to talk to me about becoming their manager. I asked him who had given the permission for him to call me and he told me it was our Chairman. So I called Thompson and he said that he thought I might be interested!

I told him that in that case I'd speak to Wolves because as far as I was concerned he'd made his position perfectly clear, but I turned the job down because I was happy where I was, we were seventh in The Premiership at the time. I then asked for a new contract, along with my staff, but he didn't want to do that either, so it was obvious, the writing was on the wall."

You mention that you felt Rodney Marsh could have been used as part of a plot to get you to leave QPR, but what are your thoughts of him as a team mate?

"Well I was much younger than Rodney, his heyday was in the Third Division really - I think he only scored three or four goals for Rangers at the highest level. He had a fantastic record in the lower division though, then after a few injury problems, did well in the Second Division team that got promoted to the top flight.

But in my opinion, the best player we had in that position, by a long way, came along after Rodney had left to join Manchester City - Stan Bowles.

But what Rodney did was to give the club a lift and the fans an idol. It was fantastic for the club to have that focus, he scored a great goal in the League Cup Final and he was a showman. Rodney was just as happy to nut-meg someone and have a laugh about it as he was to win the game, he had fantastic ability and certainly helped put the club on the map. He did an awful lot for QPR."

When Rodney left and Stan came in, did the rest of the squad feel that Bowles would fill his shoes quite so quickly?

"Well that didn't happen overnight, but I hit it off with Stan in training straight away, it was an almost telepathic relationship.

Not only that but Stan was a winner. He had his problems, whether they be gambling or not turning up, but he had outstanding ability and wanted to win games. You wouldn't think he possessed the kind of professionalism that he did, in many ways he was a 'live for today' kind of guy, always broke, always struggling for money, always borrowing money, always betting - but somehow he'd shake all that off and go out and perform.

You don't realise it at the time, but the few years I spent with Stan were the greatest in my career - we should have won the title in 1975-76, we were the best team in the country, no doubt about it."

Does that season haunt you?

"Yeah, it does a bit. Mainly because of the way the title was decided and

2002: Gerry relaxed after the interview in Surrey

the fact it wouldn't be allowed today, Liverpool playing their final fixture after we'd completed ours. We'd pushed so hard to win the Championship. I remember playing Arsenal in our penultimate home match, we knew we had to win to stay in the title race but went 1-0 down with only seven minutes to go.

Frank McLintock equalised with only two minutes on the clock, we kicked off, Stan Bowles got the ball, dribbled into the box then went down under a challenge. The referee gave a penalty. So this was it, I was the penalty taker and I knew that I was in effect taking it for QPR's chance to win The Championship .

On the front cover of the programme that day was a photo of me taking a penalty two weeks before against Wolves and it showed me putting the kick to the 'keeper's left. Loftus Road was packed to the rafters that day [30,000] and Jimmy Rimmer was in goal for Arsenal.

I walked up, put the ball down, I turned around to walk back and saw Phil Parkes at the other end of the pitch covering his eyes and looking away. Then I realised most of my other team mates were too - I thought 'thanks lads, no pressure then!'

I decided to put the ball in the opposite corner to the Wolves game, Jimmy Rimmer dived to the left and I put the ball to the right - the place went mad. They thought Stan had dived and there was almost a riot after the match.

Then we beat Leeds 2-0 in our final home match, but Liverpool weren't playing their final game that day because they were playing in the European Cup Final. It would never be allowed today and it was a terrible feeling not knowing if we were Champions or not.

I went into the TV studios to watch the Wolves-Liverpool decider, Wolves went ahead, then after what seemed a very long time, Liverpool equalised. All that we'd achieved that season, all that effort, disappeared before my eyes, I was so depressed. It meant so much to me."

You scored the Goal of the Season in 1975-76 in the opening day win over Liverpool at Loftus Road - can you talk us through the goal?

"One of the things I remember about that goal most was the fact that Phil Parkes started the move and not one Liverpool player touched it before it hit the back of the net.

Phil rolled it out to Dave Clement, Dave played it into Don Masson, he played it up to Stan Bowles who made a dummy to Don, who played it to me, I played a one-two and was clean through to slot it past Ray Clemence. It really was an excellently worked goal and we played ever so well that day. Mickey Leach got the second goal, I curled in a cross for him to score. That result proved to us that we were capable of beating anyone."

After beating Liverpool on the opening day did the press start to tout Rangers as title contenders?

Well you have to remember that during that era QPR were the best team in London by some way, it was only West Ham that used to give us close games. Teams like Arsenal, Tottenham and Chelsea were struggling then and the press did take us seriously, but whether they thought we could win the title or not I'm not so sure. Football-wise we played as close to the top European sides of that time as there was in England."

You can tell how well respected that team was, most of the players are still household names today.

"There were some fantastic individuals in the side, players that were not only skillful but also great thinkers. You've also got to remember that a lot of the important players we had there had come from the lower levels or weren't fancied by the top sides. Stan Bowles had been chucked out of two or three clubs, we picked Phil Parkes up from Walsall, Don Masson had been in the lower divisions for quite a few years, Frank McLintock was supposed to be past it and Dave Webb didn't have a lot of pace left."

You missed almost two seasons through injury after that traumatic finale, that must have been hard to take too? How did you actually get the back injury?

"I was playing against Newcastle that season on what was a completely frozen pitch. They wouldn't let horses on grass like that these days, let alone footballers. I went up for a header from a corner but I was so close to two of the Newcastle defenders that I couldn't move my hands down to break my fall and I landed right on the coxis of my lower back. It was really bad for a few days because I had moved my spine and I had shooting pains down my legs. Not many back specialists knew anything about referred pain, so I was being treated for calf strains and hamstring pulls. But looking back at the way injuries were treated then compared to what the players of today enjoy, it's shocking.

During the course of the 1975-76 season, apart from the treatment I was getting at the club, I was being pumped full of cortisone painkillers before, during and after every England game. They advise you not to use those now, so God knows what effect that's had on me.

What my back really needed was rest, but when the season was over I was picked as Captain for England's Home International campaign, then, following that, I flew out for the Bicentennial tour of America. England played against Brazil, Italy and Team America in New York, Los Angeles and Philadelphia. After that I flew to Helsinki for a World Cup qualifier. Remember, this was supposed to be the close season! We beat Finland 4-1 in what was my final England game, I had three days rest, then flew to Majorca where Rangers played against a Barcelona side that included Johan Cruyff and Johan Neeskens. But I couldn't play because my back was so sore and I didn't play again for almost two years."

Did you ever consider your back trouble may threaten your career?

"The biggest worry was that there seemed to be no cure and after I'd spent three months laying flat in bed I did start to worry about whether or not I was ever going to get better. Laying flat was fine, but as soon as I got up I got the pains shooting down my leg again. I had traction, manipulation under anaesthetic, acupuncture - I had everything. You imagine, I was the captain of both England and QPR with every specialist there was at my disposal, so in the end I was frightened to death.

I wasn't allowed to use Chiropractors and Osteopaths because in 1976 they weren't acknowledged by the insurance companies and in the end I went to see a guy called Campbell Connolly who was a Neurosurgeon and he decided to operate on my back. He told me he couldn't do the surgery for four weeks because he was going away on holiday but even afterwards there was only a 50-50 chance that I'd ever play again.

I drove back home after the meeting, parked the car, got out and shut the door, then walked back to bolt the gates. I must have left the handbrake off because as I looked round the car was coming towards me and it crushed me against the gates. That made my back a million times worse and I was in complete agony that night, so much so that my agent at the time, a guy called Ken Adam, persuaded me to see an Osteopath no matter what the implications were.

When the guy showed up the next morning he manipulated me for a while, then said he reckoned he'd have me playing in two weeks! He said I'd trapped my sciatic nerve and it was swollen. But I was still really skeptical, but he said if I wasn't playing in a fortnight I didn't have to pay him. He came every day, but my back seemed to be getting worse and I didn't know if I should carry on seeing him. Then, after the sixth day, I was starting to move easier and was able to bend slightly. He was right, I played for QPR reserves two weeks later at Bath and I had to pay him! But I was delighted and I still see him to this day.

The funny thing was, none of the other medical people I was seeing asked him what he did, how such a turn-around had been achieved or whether they could learn anything from him. If I'd had the operation I may never have played again."

Being England Captain at just twenty-three years of age which must have been amazing. Did you have to change as a person?

"Yeah, I think I did. Before that stage I had a reputation, rightly or wrongly, as being a bit of a playboy with the ladies because I had been dating and photographed with page three girls for the newspapers. They were paying me fortunes to do the pictures, but my football career was going well so I thought it was fine.

Then when I became Captain of England, Christ, every newspaper in the world came down on me and said I should be doing this or not doing that. Posing with bare breasted women was a right no-no and I was slaughtered all of a sudden.

Obviously you have to be more responsible when you become England Captain, I agree, you become a role model, so I made a concession. I carried on doing the pictures but I made the girls wear something! I was constantly compared to Bobby Moore's dignified style.

The other thing I noticed was at away grounds, one minute you're an up-and-coming England player who everyone liked and was clapped, then people started to boo me. Every time I touched the ball they jeered which was really hard to understand. But the biggest change in my life was the fact that I couldn't do anything or go anywhere without media attention. There wasn't the same exposure on television that there is now, but the newspaper attention was unbelievable, if players were spotted coming out of a nightclub on a Saturday night there would be a photo of them in *the News of the World* the next morning.

Then there was one situation, which was definitely staged, where I was asked to pose for a photograph for a man who was opening a gun shop. As soon as I picked the gun up the police turned up and arrested me, all the photographers were at the scene within seconds and I was carted off in a police car - it was unbelievable.

I guess that pressure was a lot for a twenty-three year old to cope with, especially when on top of all that I picked up the back injury and missed two years of my career."

When you eventually recovered from your back troubles, you only returned to the first team for a short while before you moved on to Crystal Palace. What made you transfer clubs?

"The situation was that my contract was finished and Rangers had just got relegated. But the biggest thing that changed my attitude about staying at QPR was the sale of Phil Parkes. I'd been at a top club, we'd nearly won the league, I'd been Captain of England, then badly injured, so I was desperate to come back and do well again.

I think the climate changed at QPR when they sold Phil and it's been the same ever since in terms of being a selling club. I remember pleading with Jim Gregory not to sell Phil Parkes because we'd already lost the likes of Frank McLintock and Webby without replacing them with any real quality and I felt the club needed to start spending money, but we didn't. Phil could have stayed with Rangers for another fifteen years. But from my personal point of view after all I'd achieved I didn't want to be playing Second Division football.

Despite my injury I felt I'd been very loyal to Rangers. Just think of it this way; as England and Queen's Park Rangers Captain at such a young age, do you think that my agent would have allowed me to stay at a club the size of Rangers in this day and age? It just wouldn't happen.

I was always happy to stay before then, but at that stage I didn't see that there would be much money spent on building that team up again. So I saw my contract out.

Did you know that I signed a contract with both Manchester United and Manchester City before Jim Gregory tore up both contracts? There was no freedom of contract then and Jim had the final say. So after agreeing personal terms and passing medicals with both Manchester clubs Jim refused to let me go and was starting to drive me mad.

I remember saying to him 'you don't want to lose me but you were happy to let Phil go'. There was even a lot of trouble with him letting me go to Crystal Palace, but in the end he got £465,000 and I spent eighteen months at Selhurst Park with Terry Venables before he came back to QPR."

From a player's point of view Jim Gregory seemed to have a very unique relationship with his team. Do you think that kind of closeness would be possible at a modern day football club?

"No, it would be impossible to have that kind of bond today. He was a unique man from that point of view and I don't think he was the same after he sold QPR. I never thought he'd actually do it, never.

I saw him at Portsmouth a few times, in fact his son offered me the manager's job down there at one stage, but I think a piece of Jim had been lost and he wasn't the same after he left Rangers."

Can you talk us through QPR's nerve-racking finish to the 1998-99 season?

"Everyone now knows the financial restrictions the club were facing when I came back as Manager, in fact I was a bit silly to come back with Rangers bottom of the league as the only person who was going to get stick if things didn't turn around was me. But I just couldn't sit back and watch that happen without trying to help.

We had a great start after I arrived and I won Manager of the Month early on but after a good little run we lost a few again and survival went to the wire. Luckily we escaped by the skin of our teeth in the final game of the season even though we won the game 6-0, but that's something I never want to go through again.

It meant so much to me to come through that situation and I'll always remember the way the players battled that day, especially Danny Maddix who played injured.

When I walked into the dressing room before the match I could feel the players' nervousness and I said that all that was expected of them was to go out and do their best. I tried to get them to relax and not worry about the magnitude of the game, I knew they wouldn't be able to play if they had the full weight of the club's fate on their shoulders."

1995: Ferdinand celebrates his second goal against Newcastle United

Les Ferdinand

Date: Thursday 31st October, 2002
Venue: West Lodge Park Hotel, Herts
Era: 1987-1995 Appearances: 170 Goals: 90

When Les Ferdinand joined Queen's Park Rangers from Hayes in April 1987, it wouldn't be too harsh to say that he was hardly an over night sensation. It took four years, two loan spells away from the club and four managers before Rangers got the best out of this promising rookie.

The supporters that would eventually idolise 'Sir Les' were hardly convinced in the early days, he was on the receiving end of a lot of stick and admits now that he found the step up to league football a massive challenge. However, an unexpected opportunity presented itself to young Les and Turkish side Besiktas took him on a year-long loan deal which was, in Les' own words, "the making of him". He returned a different player and once Gerry Francis arrived on the scene his career sky-rocketed beyond anyone's imagination.

The boy with bags of potential went on to become one of the most prolific goal-scorers ever to grace Loftus Road and one of only a handful of footballers to have represented England whilst playing for QPR. His name is now mentioned in the same breath as those of Rodney Marsh and Stan Bowles and of course he went on to earn Rangers a record six million pound transfer fee when he moved to Newcastle in 1995.

The goals he scored for QPR were vital and the rate at which he scored them had not been witnessed at The Bush for many, many years. His finest season came in 1992-93 when Les' twenty-four goals helped Rangers to a stunning fifth place finish in the Premier League. A fine performance by Les and a magnificent achievement for the club. Of course Rangers struggled to replace those goals once he left, but the respect with which fans remember him has never diminished.

The expression "you can take the player out of the club, but you can never take the club out of the player" is very apt with Les, he has never forgotten where he came from and is often found at Loftus Road cheering on the R's when Tottenham aren't playing. Ferdinand also recently made a generous and sizable donation to the We Are QPR supporters' project.

It's clear from talking to Les that he thoroughly enjoyed his good times at the club and whilst he could have moved on a lot sooner, as he says, "he never regretted the decision to stay". Ferdinand is always assured a warm reception (and usually a goal!) whenever he returns to QPR.

Les didn't want to be drawn about rumours linking him with a return to Loftus Road, but let's just say he didn't exactly rule the possibility out!

Did your move from Hayes to Rangers seem a massive one?

"It did, it took me quite a while to become accustomed to the move and settle down I think. One minute I was buying football magazines at the newsagents and reading about other players, the next I was picking them up and seeing my photo inside. It really was a major step for me and a lot of my friends were kicking themselves. I'd played non-league football with a lot of my mates, but after parties and girls came into play, quite a few fell by the wayside."

Your move proved to be a fantastic bit of business by Hayes, especially when you subsequently moved from QPR to Newcastle. They must be delighted with you?

"Without a shadow of a doubt, they got 10% of the £6m that Rangers were paid and they made a good deal of money at a time when the club was going through some financial difficulties."

Did it feel good to know that you were helping your old club out as you moved up the ladder personally?

"Well, kind of, yeah. The thing is I'd only been at Hayes for about six months, so it wasn't as if I'd been there years and years and felt I owed Hayes a debt."

You didn't serve a traditional footballer's apprenticeship so what was it like to suddenly be training every day at a full time club and have Jim Smith as manager?

"I found the step up very difficult, but Jim was always very supportive. I'd only been at Rangers for a couple of months before I got an opportunity to travel with the first team to see what it was really all about.

I'd been scoring quite a few goals in the reserves and Jim decided to give me a little taster. He took me to one side before an away game at Wimbledon and said 'you're not going to be involved in the game, but I want you to come along with the first team and see how we do things'. I remember meeting at Loftus Road, we had a pre-match meal and travelled to the match by coach - I was like a little kid, wide-eyed and excited."

Were you made to feel at home?

"They were all really good to me yeah. [Laughs] To be honest I got involved with the Rangers 'Brat Pack' which at the time included players like Clive Walker, Dave Kerslake and Gary Chivers.

Those guys wanted to leave the club and were a bit rebellious. Somehow I found myself in with them and we got into a few scrapes. I was the rebel without a cause for a while."

I guess your year loan move to Turkey broke your involvement with that crew?

"Jim Smith told me he believed in me and thought I was going to do well, but he thought I needed to get away from the influences which I had in my every day life. He said he had a mate out in Turkey who needed a centre-forward and asked if I'd be interested in going out there. I said that I would be, but at the time I was just humouring him really.

Then one day after training he pulled me to one side and said the guy from Besiktas had been watching me train, a bloke called Gordon Milne. So I had a little chat with him and he sold me on the opportunity of playing regular first team football in front of real crowds and learning the ropes.

Gordon was such a nice fella and the way he described things really appealed to me, so I went straight home and told my Mum that I was going off to Turkey for a year. For Jim Smith to be offering me the opportunity it meant that I wasn't really going to figure in his short term plans anyway."

It proved to be a wise move didn't it?

"To be totally honest, it was the making of me, it was the apprenticeship I never had. I couldn't speak the language that well so all I could do was play and concentrate on football. The coaching was great too, Gordon Milne took me under his wing over there and was fantastic to me. He played a big part in making me what I am today."

You must have returned a far more confident player, how did Rangers deal with you when you arrived back in England?

"Well, the move had been working out so well that Gordon and I flew back to England when Trevor Francis took over from Jim Smith. We wanted to talk to Trevor about extending the loan if possible.

Francis said that he was aware how well things were going, but he didn't want to prolong the deal, he added that if they wanted to buy me they could though - he was willing to sell me. At the time Turkish clubs didn't really pay transfer fees for players, the culture was the better players would be attracted to the bigger clubs because they were paid more money but there wasn't a transfer system as such.

Trevor Francis said the club would accept £500,000 for me, but refused the option of another loan. In the end I came back and resumed training at Rangers and started to do well."

The first turning point at Rangers was your brace against Chelsea in the 4-2 win at Loftus Road in December 1989 wasn't it?

"Yeah, that came out of the blue really. I'd been scoring goals in the reserves, then I came in from training one Friday and the manager told me

I was in the squad. Then, when I arrived at the ground the next day, Trevor told me I was playing. Francis was going through a bit of a tough time then, results weren't really going his way."

The fact that the goals were against Chelsea must have made that day a very special one for you?

"Well, it wasn't until that day that I realised how important beating Chelsea was to Queen's Park Rangers' fans. Being a black kid from Ladbroke Grove, I didn't really go to football because of the racist problems so I wasn't aware of the importance of the fixture really. But those goals almost made me a hero over-night, it was fantastic."

Despite the win against Chelsea, Trevor Francis got the sack shortly afterwards. How did that affect you?

"Well it was a pretty turbulent time for me. Don Howe took over and he signed Roy Wegerle. I remember up at Sheffield just after Roy arrived when Don made me the scapegoat for the team's poor first half display - he came in at half-time and said he wanted to make some changes. Then he said, 'Les, you're playing like you're waiting for someone to take your place', then he took me off for Roy.

Ray Wilkins came over to me afterwards and said how out of order he thought Don had been and how badly he'd handled things. He told me to keep my chin up because he thought I'd been doing well and had been unfairly singled out."

Was that incident a blow to your confidence?

"It did affect me, yes. Don Howe had let it be known that Mark Falco and Roy Wegerle were going to be his main strike partnership because he felt Mark and myself couldn't play together. And, as QPR had just paid £1m for Roy, he was obviously going to play ahead of me, so I went through the rest of the season stuck on the sub's bench. I also remember that I took a bit of stick from the supporters at the time too, I got the impression that they felt I wasn't living up to my potential and were disappointed with my performances. So it wasn't always rosy at QPR for me."

So what changed and triggered your transformation at Rangers?

"It was Gerry Francis' arrival really but my form came good at the same time too. It was coming to the end of the 1990-91 season and both Falco and Wegerle got injured, I remember playing a game at Luton on the Astro-turf and Don Howe decided to play me up front with Bradley Allen. We won the game 2-1, I scored two and then things started to change. I went on a goal-scoring spree after that, scoring seven goals in nine games.

That was my first extended run in the side and I was able to stay injury free as well. We just about avoided relegation that season, but during the summer Howe was sacked and Gerry took over.

After he joined Gerry told me that he'd tried to sign me a couple of times while he was at Bristol Rovers and how much he admired me as a player. He also told me that he would not only get me playing in the Rangers first team, but he thought he could get me into the England team too.

He really instilled confidence in me, but to be honest, things still didn't work out straight away. I was still in and out of the side and I was still getting stick from some supporters. Then things clicked all of a sudden and I was able to reproduce my training ground form every Saturday."

So Gerry Francis was very good news for Les Ferdinand?

"Without a doubt, Gerry helped me to make it in this country. It was a bit of a disappointment that I couldn't join him when he took over at Tottenham really, as I'd already shaken hands with Kevin Keegan on a deal to go up to Newcastle. Then a couple of days later Gerry called me from Tottenham and asked me if I wanted to go to White Hart Lane. I said if he'd phoned me two days earlier the answer would have been yes, but I like to think I'm a man of my word and I do what I say I'm going to do."

You had a period over Easter 1993 where everything seemed to be going right for you, scoring back-to-back hat-tricks two days apart, then called up to the England squad. Do you consider that time to be THE Les Ferdinand purple patch?

"People always say to me that they think I was at my best when I played for Newcastle. I had a fantastic time up there and my goals-to-games ratio was more impressive, but I think at Rangers I wasn't just scoring goals, I was also playing extremely well.

At Newcastle I had a supply line, David Ginola and Keith Gillespie were told by Keegan that it was their jobs to feed me crosses. When I went to Newcastle, gone were the days where I would pick the ball up then have to beat two or three players but at QPR that was part of my game. My mates used to turn round to me and say 'what's up with you Les, you don't run with the ball any more, all you do is hit the back of the net...'

But I was playing as a lone striker up there a lot of the time, with my back to goal and I was able to feed off some great crosses. So yes, I would say that period at QPR was the best period I've enjoyed as a player."

Do you remember those hat-tricks vividly?

"I do, yeah! The first was against Nottingham Forest, it was a cracking game. That's something else I remember about that era at Rangers, there

1993: Les sniffing goals during the 2-1 win at Villa Park

2002: Les Ferdinand poses after the interview in Cockfosters

were always ding-dong, high scoring matches. I got my hat-trick with a diving header inside the six-yard box right at the end of the game to make it 4-3 to Rangers.

The next one was at Goodison Park against Everton and the Rangers team were amazing that day, the win certainly wasn't all about me though - Andy Impey cut inside and scored a cracker into the top corner and that got us going. A few QPR players scored hat-tricks against Everton in the space of a couple of seasons - Andy Sinton, myself and Bradley Allen.

I've often said that I received a lot of racial abuse at Goodison Park so I always have an extra determination to score against Everton.

Peter Beardsley played in that Everton side and when we teamed up at Newcastle we started talking about it. He said that before the game the Everton manager, Howard Kendall, had told his players to kick me up in the air early and try and put me off my game. [Laughs] I remember being clattered early on, but they just couldn't cope with me that day. Kendall said after the match that if he ever told his players to kick someone in future, they should turn round and tell him to shut up!"

You always seemed to have an ability to hang in the air longer than it seemed humanly possible. How do you manage that?
"[Laughs] I really don't know, I suppose it's all down to timing. I'm just bordering six feet tall and I can out-jump people who are a lot bigger than me, but I've always had this in-built knack and it comes naturally to me."

You mention the racial abuse you got from Everton fans, how bad was it?
"Well it was the first club I'd got it from. I've had letters and messages on my website saying that I always give Everton a hard time, but when people have asked me where the worst abuse I've received was, I tell them.

I've scored more goals against Everton than against any other club in the league and that added incentive for me, because of the grief I've got, has played a part in getting my goals I'm sure. I would not only hear people shout racist stuff at me from the stands, but I would open my mail on a Monday or Tuesday morning after playing up there and find letters with Swastikas on - that's why I am still quite vocal about them."

You scored on your England debut as a Rangers player, what did that feel like?
"It was really funny, my rise from doing well in the league for QPR and being called up for England was very, very quick. I'd just signed a new contract with the club three weeks before and in it was a clause that said if I was ever called up, the deal would have to be renegotiated.

I was lucky though, my good form coincided with other strikers' injuries. My first call-up was for a match against Turkey, but I wasn't involved in the game. Then I was called up for the San Marino match, I trained well and Graham Taylor told me I was playing.

I thought I was going to be really nervous, but on the day I felt really cool, I listed to my music before the match and it wasn't the daunting prospect I thought it would be. Unfortunately there was a lot of pressure to score plenty of goals and we were expected to win heavily.

One of my biggest memories of the game wasn't that we won though, it was the grief that John Barnes got from some of the crowd - after all he'd done for England. Unfortunately that was the memory I took away from the game, not that I'd performed well and scored on my debut."

The press must have been all over you at the time, how did you cope with that?

"I still struggle to cope with it now to be honest, I just see myself as a normal guy doing a job that I'm privileged to be doing. The job certainly gives you perks and we all love it when people are printing nice things about us, [laughs] the problem is when they're not so nice about you. But the day you play for England your profile in the press rockets and that's what happened to me, almost over night."

Then Rangers went and finished fifth in the Premiership.

"Well just look back at the team we had that season, it was a really good side and we competed with the best of them. QPR were never going to be a side that won the league that season but in London we became everyone's second-best team - barring Chelsea fans obviously. We were a tremendous footballing side that year."

There was talk of you leaving Rangers before the start of the 1994-95 season though, what was it that made you stay for one more year?

"When I spoke to the Chairman about leaving there was a lot of talk about me going to Arsenal. Gerry Francis was the biggest influence in me staying though, also I had the feeling that I didn't feel I'd improved sufficiently as a player the season before. I thought the time wasn't necessarily right for me to move on and I guess I stayed so that I could improve.

People have said to me that with hindsight I should have left Rangers sooner, but my only regret is that I haven't won more things in football. If I'd left Queen's Park Rangers earlier, then maybe I would have achieved that, but then again, maybe I wouldn't.

I never regret the decision to stay, I enjoyed my time at Rangers and football has been very good to me."

So when Newcastle came in for you a year later, the time was then right to move on?

"Yes it was, but if the supporters are honest with themselves, a lot of them were saying the same thing too. Yes Les Ferdinand had been good for Queen's Park Rangers, but people were saying that £6m was too much to turn down and I think that's why I get such a warm reception when I come back."

What was your first return to Loftus Road like as a Newcastle player?

"It was so fantastic, I was really choked. I remember getting away from Danny Maddix, who did a very good job on me that day, and scored. After the game Danny said, 'Les, I knew you were quick, but I didn't know you were that quick.'

[Laughs] When I went to my Dad's house later that night he showed me all the local 'papers and there was a photo of Danny Maddix with boxing gloves on saying how he was going to shackle me during the game. That really made me laugh."

What did you feel when Rangers got relegated in your first season away while you were finishing runners-up with Newcastle?

"A lot of people tried to make out that it was only my goals that had kept Rangers up in the past, but I think that is really unfair on all the other players. It was heartbreaking to see because QPR will always have a place in my heart, I'll always have an affinity with Rangers. Who knows, I may even play for them again one day?"

1975: Stan looks pleased with himself after being called up for England

Stan Bowles

Date: Thursday 17th October, 2002
Venue: The New England Pub, Brentford
Era: 1972-1979 Appearances: 315 Goals: 96

Stan started his career at Manchester City, moving onto Bury, Crewe and Carlisle before arriving at Loftus Road for a £112,000 fee, which was arguably a large gamble on a player who many considered temperamental. But the maverick forward, who had failed at four clubs before arriving, came of age at Loftus Road - Stan not only ably filled Rodney Marsh's boots but also made that number ten shirt his own too.

Bowles was a special player and he doesn't really get the credit he deserves - many people believe that he should be talked about in the same breath as George Best and they are probably not wrong. Bowles was, quite simply put, one of the most brilliant, exciting and unique footballers this country has ever produced.

Meeting Stan I was expecting a no-holds-barred evening and that's exactly what I got! There is no messing around with Stan, no dodging questions, if you ask him something, you get a direct answer and I found that very refreshing and extremely entertaining!

No disrespect intended but he sounds like an absolute nightmare to manage, he always did what he wanted regardless of what he was told or who told him traits which are further underlined in this interview. I think it's to Jim Gregory's and Dave Sexton's credit that they managed to get the best out of the man where so many had failed before.

It would be very easy to be judgemental and critical of Stan, some would probably wonder what sort of player he would have been had he not had so many demons. Personally I think that's irrelevant because after speaking to so many of his team-mates, it's clear that whatever was going on with Stan off the pitch, once that whistle went, he was all business and able to turn it on at the drop of a hat. It's also clear that Stan was a great team player and wanted desperately to win every game. Having never seen him play that was never my preconception and I'm delighted to have been but right about that.

Meeting Stan was one of the best days of my life and everyone reading this book will understand just why Stan Bowles was such a terrace hero and why he is still stopped in the streets over twenty years after retiring from the game.

Every genius has his flaws, and Stan had plenty of those, but he was OUR genius! He meant so much to Rangers back then and today his legend transcends generations - I hope the interview does him justice.

You'd already played for Manchester City, Bury, Crewe and Carlisle before you joined Rangers, so did you see QPR as a place to settle down when you arrived?

"All I really wanted when I left Carlisle was to go to a London club and Rangers were the first ones to come in. I was supposed to join Stoke City, their manager at the time, Tony Waddington, was after me.

But I'd got it into my head to go to London because that's where the money was and when I came up to Shepherd's Bush for talks we got the deal done and dusted within a day."

Rangers bought you as Rodney Marsh's replacement, was it daunting having to emulate such a crowd favourite?

"No, because at the end of the day I'd never heard of Rodney Marsh. It was just a total coincidence really, I was playing up north and I hadn't heard of him, I expect he'd never heard of me either. When I arrived at QPR nobody wanted to wear Rodney's number ten shirt, but I said 'I'll wear it', because I'd never heard of him."

Your career really took off after joining QPR and you went on to star in the First Division runners-up team. You then became our leading scorer in the subsequent UEFA Cup run, then got picked to represent England before moving to Nottingham Forest in a big money transfer. Did you ever think you'd have that level of success in the game?

"No, not really, but I didn't really give a fuck, as far as I was concerned people could take me or leave me.

There were a lot of good, established players at the club when I arrived, players like Terry Venables. But I just got on with doing my own thing which took a few people aback I think. They tried to get me to do this and that, but I did what I wanted.

The best manager I've ever had was Dave Sexton, but even he couldn't tell me what to do. But within hours of joining I'd met Gerry Francis and we knew we could work well together straight away, it was amazing, he knew what I was going to do and I knew what he was going to do - it's called being good footballers."

Do you remember anything about your debut?

"Funny enough it was against Notts. Forest, I scored a header from a Don Givens corner in a 3-0 win. I think that helped the crowd warm to me straight away. I remember doing a few tricks and that, like Rodney Marsh used to do, then they took to me.

Once you get that initial goal you start to get the confidence and I felt at home from game one onwards.

In the end I could get away with anything at Rangers because the crowd liked me so much, even if I was playing badly they'd blame someone else. If I messed up all I had to do was look at the crowd, shrug my shoulders and smile as if to say 'what more can I do?' then they'd have a go at David Webb or someone else!

I used to do it on purpose if I made a bad pass which used to aggravate the other players at times. [Laughs] Tough shit though, I'd rather have the crowd booing them than me!"

Did the other players have words with you after the game when that happened - did they pull you up for it?

"[Laughs] Yeah a few of them asked me what I was playing at, but I used to say I didn't know what they were talking about.

David Webb and Frank McLintock were too stressed anyway, before the games they were a bag of nerves. Unlike the others I used to get into the dressing room ten minutes before kick-off, but one day Dave Sexton turned round and told me that all the other players were getting the needle.

I said 'Dave, it only takes me two minutes to put on my shirt, shorts and tie my boots up - tell the others to stop panicking and let's get on with it'. That was the end of it, he never mentioned it again after that.

David and Frank would be at the ground an hour and a half before the game, warming up and doing stretches, but I wasn't in to all that and I didn't do too bad did I?"

You scored four hat-tricks at QPR; against Swindon, Derby and two in the UEFA Cup. Which one was the best?

"It was probably the double hat-trick against the Norwegian club Brann Bergen because that was in Europe. The foreign sides weren't as good back then as they are now, but I still got a hat-trick in both legs, which was special."

The players that have been interviewed for this book who played with yourself and Rodney have all been asked to compare the two of you. They all said that you were both very gifted, but that you were the less selfish player - are they correct?

"It's a fair comment yes, but it doesn't answer the question that you were trying to ask them does it? What you were really trying to find out was if they thought he was a better player than me, wasn't it? Personally, I don't think he was to be honest.

I could do all the same little tricks he did, anyone can show off to the crowd. But you've got to work for the team too. Rodney only played in the lower leagues with QPR anyway."

After all these years do you find the constant comparisons between the two of you annoying?

"Not really, no. It doesn't bother me, because there isn't a comparison in my mind."

There were obviously a lot of great Rangers performances the season we finished second in the First Division, do you have a favourite?

"No, not really. People say we lost the Championship that year when we lost against Norwich, but I think we really lost the title by drawing silly games earlier in the season. But we were definitely the best side in the country that season, we were better than Liverpool without a doubt.

I remember when we played Norwich we were still 5-1 on to win the First Division, I ask you, when will QPR ever get those odds on winning The Premiership again?"

After we'd beaten Leeds and completed our fixtures that season, we had a long wait to learn our fate. What was the mood like among the squad?

"Well it couldn't happen now, everyone would be made to complete their fixtures on the same day.

Gerry Francis and me went in to the BBC studios to watch the Liverpool-Wolves match that night, but after Liverpool equalised I knew it was only a matter of time. We knew that one point wouldn't have been enough anyway.

That result cost me £6,000, which was a lot of money back then. I went down to the pub outside the studios and got drunk. It wasn't the money though, I wanted to win the Championship for the Chairman, Jim Gregory, who I was very close to."

You wanted to win the league more for Chairman Jim Gregory than Manager Dave Sexton then?

"Yeah. When I arrived at Rangers I thought Dave was very boring - Dave's a good friend of mine now, but I didn't like him at first. He made us stand around listening to complicated manoeuvres and all that - he wanted us to be playing like the Dutch, but all I wanted to do was fuck about.

He used to go on about the forwards tracking back, that was a bone of contention between me and Dave, he used to say 'you just don't want to listen to me do you Stan?' I used to tell him, 'I'll listen to you Dave, but at the end of the day, I know best'.

I'm not stupid, I would take in what he was telling me, some things he said were right, but I'd never admit it. [Laughs] I used to drive him crazy on matchdays, he used to take me to one side and tell me what he wanted me to do, I would agree to whatever he said, then just go out on the pitch and do whatever I wanted anyway.

But when I got round to thinking about it, he was right, he was way ahead of his time which is why he's still involved in the England scouting set up to this day at the age of seventy."

You had a very good relationship with Jim Gregory. Did your friendship annoy the other team members?

"Yeah, it was normally a good relationship, either I got money off of him or I didn't! I think it did upset a few of the lads though, I was getting £200 in cash off the Chairman every Monday morning and people like Don Masson weren't happy about it when they found out.

Don went in to Gregory when he found out and told him that he wanted £200 too, but Jim told him 'well, you're not as good as Stan, so fuck off!' [Laughs] And Don was Captain of Scotland!

Half the players liked me, half didn't, but to tell you the truth I didn't care what they thought, those little jealousy things always happen in football. I doubt I would have enjoyed myself at Rangers if it weren't for Jim though."

You blossomed under Dave Sexton but it was Gordon Jago who signed you. How do you compare the two managers?

"Gordon signed quite a few good players for Rangers to be fair, but he was a completely different bloke to Sexton.

Gordon always used to panic, every time he got into a problem with me he used to get a red eye, like when I walked out on the England squad.

I remember Gordon wrote to me a few years back, it said that even after all the trouble I'd caused him, he still loved me!"

You also played under Alec Stock, did you get on with him?

"Yeah he was all right Alec. He'd had a long relationship with Rangers and we got on pretty well. In fact he used to drive me in to training every morning from Ruislip in his Triumph Stag."

How about Tommy Docherty, you weren't his biggest fan?

"Tommy wasn't my cup of tea, I thought he was an out and out liar. If he tried to tell you it was raining outside, you would always go and check the weather yourself.

It was Tommy who sold me to Nottingham Forest, when it didn't work out he said he would buy me back, but he didn't.

When I went up to Nottingham to sign, Jim Gregory phoned me and said 'if you don't want to go, don't go', but I got £47,000 cash to go there, so I

Stan Bowles, Terry Venables & Tony Hazell try out a bouncy castle

1977: Bowles & Francis in training for the League Cup Semi-Final against Aston Villa

thought I'd take a chance. In hindsight, it was the worst move I ever made, I should have stayed at Rangers. Although my popularity hasn't diminished over the years, but it could have done.

[Laughs] I suppose you want to know where the £47,000 went... Well, you tell me!"

How did you find Brian Clough?

"Cloughie was all right, when he was asleep! No, I didn't get on with him and walked out on him before the European Cup Final.

I told him he could poke his European Cup winner's medal, which he did - a kid called Gary Mills got my medal in the end.

Mills apologised a couple of years afterwards, but I told him not to be sorry, at the end of the day you can't eat medals.

I didn't dislike Clough, he was quite amusing sometimes, but there was a clash of personalities. When you see Cloughie on the telly, that's not an act you know, he really is that arrogant. In the dressing room one day I remember him saying, 'Rome wasn't built in a day, but remember this laddie, I wasn't on that job!' He was a fucking nutcase."

Rangers' European campaign in 1976-77 was fantastic for you personally wasn't it?

"Yes it was, I broke Denis Law's goal-scoring record which only John Wark [Ipswich] has ever bettered. That was the highlight of my career really and I suppose I enjoyed that season more than the runners-up campaign from a personal point of view.

My most memorable goal in Europe that year was the one against Cologne at Shepherd's Bush, that broke the record and I remember thinking, 'fucking hell!'

The best side we played in the run were Slovan Bratislava, that was a cracking tie. We drew 3-3 over there and we beat them 5-2 at home - but it really could have been 5-5. It was all out attacking football by both sides and they had nine of the Czech international squad in their side at the time.

But missing out on the Championship was a bigger heartbreak than missing out in Europe, especially for the fans."

I've read your autobiography and there are some notorious stories about your off the pitch exploits in Europe that season. Was the club petrified every time you went away?

"Not really, I was never that bad. If I wanted a drink I had a drink, if I didn't want a drink I wouldn't have one. I wasn't a heavy drinker then, but if I fancied one I'd go for it."

2002: Stan enjoys a reminisce about the good old days

You and Don Shanks seemed to be inseparable while you were both at QPR. But all those little scrapes that you talk about in your book seemed to be started by him?

"Yeah, they were, in fact he started the incident that saw me getting beaten up in a Belgian police cell. [Laughs] Dave Sexton said he originally bought Don so he could look after me!

We're talking about a manic gambler, a hundred times worse than I am, I swear to you! As far as the manager was concerned it was a move that backfired.

But it was Dave Webb who was my unofficial on the pitch minder, like that time when Webby knocked Kenny Burns out when we were playing Birmingham.

Funny enough Kenny had a go at me about that when I eventually joined up with him at Forest. [Laughs] I was a bit spiteful as a player at times, but I didn't have the strength to back it up, so when Kenny came over to get me after I'd fouled him, Webby said 'leave him to me Stan' before laying him out flat."

When you look at how modern day football stars are slaughtered by the press for similar behaviour, why do you think that yourself and George Best were always forgiven and almost idolised because of the way you behaved?

"I don't really know why, all I know is that we're both remembered more than twenty years after we've finished playing.

George is the best player I've seen in my whole life and like him I still get stopped wherever I go - it's fucking amazing.

The other week I was at QPR and this fan came over to say hello to me with his eight-year-old son.

The bloke said to his little boy, 'that's the best player we've ever had, Stan Bowles'. The little boy said, 'who's he Dad?' With that the bloke slapped his son round the back of the head and said, 'who's he?' Whack! 'You can't say things like that!' It's times like those that make me realise how special Rangers are to me."

Do you think that modern day Premiership stars will be recognised in twenty years after they've finished playing?

"No."

Photo Credits

Page	Photographer/Agency	
Ian Gillard		
10-11	EMPICS	
17	Dave Lane	
Rodney Marsh		
26-27	Ron Gould	
30	Ron Gould	
32	Colorsport	
Paul Parker		
36-37	Colousport	
44	EMPICS	
Tony Ingham		
48-49	Unknown	Ingham's personal collection
53	Unknkown	Ingham's personal collection
54	Unknown	Ingham's personal collection
56	Dave Lane	
157	Unknown	Ingham's personal collection
Mark Lazarus		
67-68	Unknown	Lazarus' personal collection
63	Dave Lane	
64-65	Ron Gould	
Terry Venables		
68-69	Colorsport	
74	EMPICS	
76	Dave Lane	
Gary Waddock		
80-81	EMPICS	
86	Colorsport	
88	Dave Lane	
Phil Parkes		
92-93	EMPICS	
96	EMPICS	
98	Dave Lane	
Alan McDonald		
102-103	EMPICS	
113	EMPICS	
114	EMPICS	
Gerry Francis		
118-119	Colorsport	
125	Dave Lane	
Les Ferdinand		
132-133	Colorsport	
139	EMPICS	
140	Dave Lane	
Stan Bowles		
144-145	EMPICS	
151	EMPICS	
152	EMPICS	
154	Dave Lane	

Record appearance holder Tony Ingham

"We're by far the greatest team, the world has ever seen..."